EMPLOYABILITY SKILLS MCQ

MANOJ DOLE

Digitization is the need of the time. In the future, training in industrial training institutes will need to be conducted using online internet to make training more convenient and easy.
E-books containing a set of MCQ questions will be made available to the trainees as they need to be more accustomed to the multiple choice questions MCQ to prepare for the online
exams taking place in their industrial training institutes.

With all these factors in mind, Mr. Manoj Madhukar Dole Instructor, Industrial Training Institute, Satara, has written books according to the new annual system and NSQF-5 syllabus. And they've created theoretical mobile apps and blogs to make training easier, and made all these educational materials available for download on the world famous websites Google Play Store, Amazon and Apple Book Store.

The books were published by Hon'ble Joint Director Shri Rajendra Ghume Saheb Regional Office of Vocational Education and Training, Pune on 9/1/2019, at this time
Shri Prakash Saigavkar Saheb Principal Government Industrial Training Institute Aundh Pune, Shri Tukaram Misal Saheb Principal Govt. Q. Sanstha Satara, Shri Sachin Dhumal Saheb District Vocational Education and Training Officer Satara, Shri Yatin Pargaonkar Saheb Principal Govt. Q. Sanstha Kolhapur, Shri Vikas Teke Saheb Inspector Vocational Education and Training Regional Office Pune, Palekar Foods Products Pvt. Ltd. Entrepreneurial Chairman of Satara Mr. Nilkanthrao Palekar Saheb, Chairman of Hira Foods Mr. Ibrahim Baba Tamboli Saheb, Mrs. Shalmali Pawar Headmaster Government Technical School Center Satara and other dignitaries were present on the occasion.

Contents

Prologue *vii*

Foreword *ix*

Preface *xi*

Acknowledgements *xiii*

1. Employability Skills Mcq E-learning 1
2. English Literacy Mcq 21
3. Entrepreneurship Skills Mcq 30
4. Productivity Mcq 34
5. Occupational Safety Mcq 44
6. Labour Welfare Legislation Mcq 55
7. Quality Tools Mcq 61
8. I.t. Literacy Mcq 70

Prologue

EMPLOYABILITY SKILLS MCQ is a simple Book for ITI Subject EMPLOYABILITY SKILLS Revised NSQF Syllabus, It contains objective questions with underlined & bold correct answers MCQ covering all topics including all about the latest & Important about-

English literacy module to understand the application of skills like pronunciation, functional grammar, greeting, introduction etc

I.T. Literacy This module covers the topics like Basics of computer, MS Word, MS Excel, Internet and Emailing etc. The IT literacy has two sections - theory and exercise. The theory section covers the basic information and application of computers.

Communication Skills This module is covering the topics like verbal communication, non verbal communication, listening, self awareness and behavioural skill etc. The communication skills module has two sections - theory and exercise. The theory section helps the trainee to understand the need of the skill, practical application and any other relevant information.

Entrepreneurship Skills It is intended for the aspiring youths who undergo technical trainings in various trades and wish to take up entrepreneurship as a career opportunity.

'Productivity' is about how well people combine resources to produce goods and services like raw material, labour, skills, capital equipment, land, intellectual property, managerial capability and financial capital.

Occupational Safety, Health and Environment Education It protects co-workers, family members, employees, customers, suppliers and others who are involved in the workplace environment.

Labour Welfare Legislation includes overall welfare facilities designed to take care of well being of employee's and in order to increase their living standard.

The quality tools given here are very important for not only providing them precise knowledge inputs but also would be able to apply problem solving techniques through development of QC for continuous improvements to become an outstanding and efficient quality personal.

We add new question answers with each new version. Please email us in case of any errors/omissions. This is arguably the largest and best Book for All engineering multiple choice questions and answers.

As a student you can use it for your exam prep. This Book is also useful for professors to refresh material.

Foreword

Vocational education and training is imparted through the Department of Vocational Education and Training through the Department of Business Education and Business Practical to supply multi-skilled artisans in line with the rapidly growing demand in the industrial sector in the 21st century. All the occupations within the institutions are important, as the trainees from these occupations develop multi-skills as per the demands of the industry.

with the noble intention of making available MCQ e-books suitable for all businesses, considering that all the examinations in all the industries in the industrial sector are conducted online and include MCQ method questions. Mr. Manoj Madhukar Dole has written a very good e-book on MCQ method as per the new annual syllabus. This e-book will definitely be a guide for all the trainees, trainee candidates, training instructors and others concerned.

The author of the book is Mr. Manoj Madhukar Dole, Instructor Gov. ITI Satara has 17 years of training experience. Written as a new annual pattern, this e-book incorporates modern digital QR Code technology to understand the layout, simple language, and simple syntax, diagrams and videos for each subject. So I am sure that this e-book will definitely be useful for in-depth study and exam practice. The work they have done is certainly commendable.

Mr. Tukaram Misal
Principal Government Industrial Training Institute Satara.

Preface

DGET New Delhi and CSTARI Kolkata have been implementing an annual pattern for all businesses in ITI since the August 2018 session. The examination system will also be changed and it will be online from this year and since all the questions are of Objective Type (MCQ), the trainees are in dire need of in-depth study. It is with this in mind that we are delighted to present the books based on the old NIMI pattern and a complete overview of the new annual pattern, and we hope that these books will be a guide for all business directors and trainees. Is.

For writing these books, Johar Awate Saheb, Principal of ITI Akluj. Former Principal of ITI Satara Saigavkar Saheb, Assistant Director Shri Chandrakant Dhekne Saheb Regional Office of Vocational Education and Training, Pune, District Vocational Education and Training Officer Sachin Dhumal Saheb and Headmaster Government Technical School Kendra Shalmali Pawar Madam and son Adhiraj Dole, mother Kusum Dole, I am very grateful to my father Madhukar Dole and wife Ashwini Dole for their special guidance and cooperation from time to time.

Also, in a very short period of time, the book was reviewed by Shri Rajendra Ghume Saheb, Joint Director, Vocational Education and Training Regional Office, Pune, for his invaluable time in publishing the book. I am sincerely grateful for their feedback.

I am grateful to the Instructor of ITI Satara for there continuous support from the very beginning of writing the book.

From this book, I consider myself blessed to have shared my thoughts on e-learning with you. I will not claim that this book is perfect, because considering the perfection, this book is an attempt and is in its infancy. They will be valuable for improvement if they are tested and suggested.

Manoj Dole
Dated 9/1/2019

Acknowledgements

The industrial training and theoretical examination system of our industrial training institutes and these changes have been accepted by the craft instructors and the trainees.

Theoretical examinations conducted in your industrial training institutes are also conducted online. Since these examinations are of multiple choice MCQ method, the trainees will need to get more practice of such questions.

With all these considerations in mind, Mr. Manoj Madhukar, Director, Dole Crafts, Katari Industrial Training Institute, Satara, has done a thorough study and with his diligent work and added his keen intellect, according to the new annual system and NSQF-5 syllabus, e-book of Katari and other machine trades. -Book) and they have created mobile apps and blogs on theoretical topics to make training easier and have made all these educational materials available for download on the world famous websites Google Play Store, Amazon and Apple Book Store. Training has been made easier by creating a print version and using advanced techniques like QR Code.

All these educational materials will definitely be a guide for all the trainees for in-depth study and for the craft instructors and other concerned who are imparting vocational training.

CHAPTER ONE

EMPLOYABILITY SKILLS MCQ e-Learning

Online Test Exam
ITI Books
CNC Course
AutoCAD CAM
JOB & Apprentice
Online Theory
Computer Course
Trading Course
Web Designing
MSCIT Course
Shopping Business
Internet Business
Remotasks Course
Online Services
Top Sportsmans
Indian Army
Freedom Fighters
Top Scientists
Social Reformers
Motivational Speaker
Top Richest People
Join WhatsApp Group
Join Facebook Group
Like Facebook Page
PAN / Adhar / Licence Passport

ई-पुस्तक प्रकाशन

English Literacy

Entrepreneurship skills

Productivity Video

Occupational safety

Labour welfare legislation

Quality tools

I.T. Literacy

COMPUTER PARTS
COMPUTER
MOUSE
KEY BOARD
SCREEN / MONITOR
FLASH DRIVE
TOWER
COMPACT DISC
LAPTOP
PRINTER
SCANNER
CARTRIDGES
WEB CAM

COMPUTER PARTS
SPEAKER
HEADPHONES
SMARTPHONE
TABLET / I-PAD
MICROPHONE
WIRELESS ROUTER
MP3 PLAYER
JOYSTICK / GAME

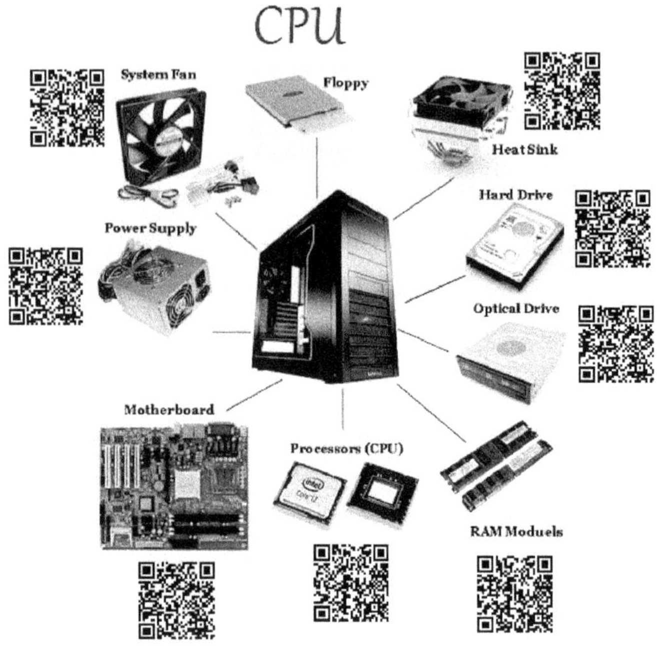

Computer CPU
Hardware Components

Motherboard
Hardware Components

Excel Basic Functions

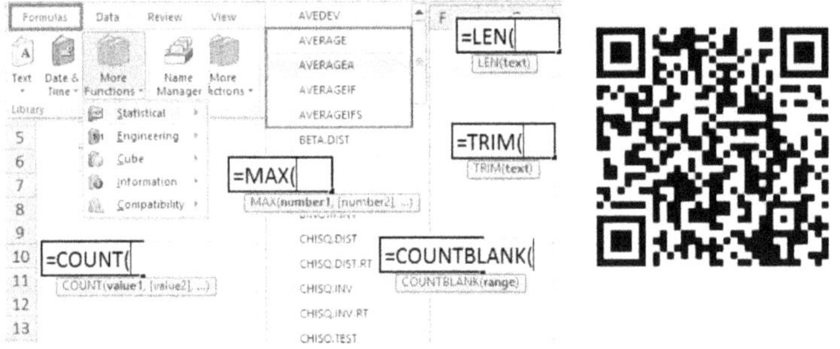

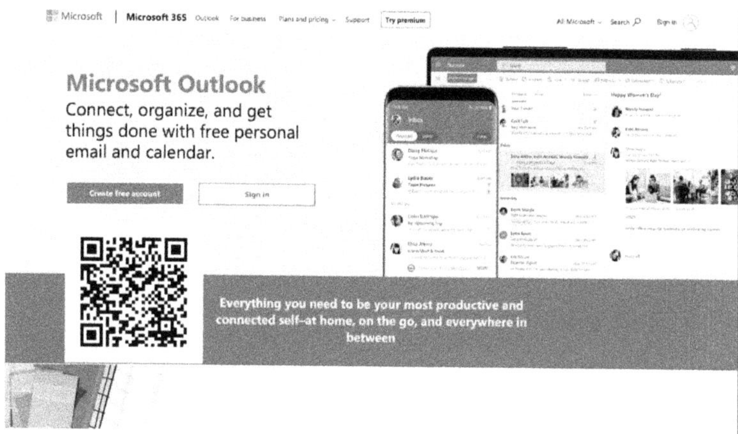
Microsoft
Microsoft 365
Try premium
Microsoft Outlook
Connect, organize, and get things done with free personal email and calendar.
Create free account
Sign in
Everything you need to be your most productive and connected self–at home, on the go, and everywhere in between

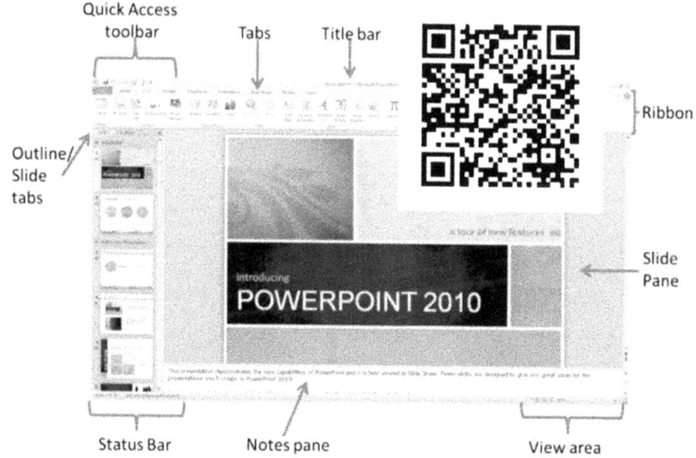
Quick Access toolbar
Tabs
Title bar
Ribbon
Outline/ Slide tabs
Slide Pane
Introducing
POWERPOINT 2010
Status Bar
Notes pane
View area

MS Paint

Microsoft
FEATURES OF
MS WORD
IN HINDI
W
• WHAT IS MS WORD
• HISTORY OF MS WORD
• FEATURES OF MS WORD

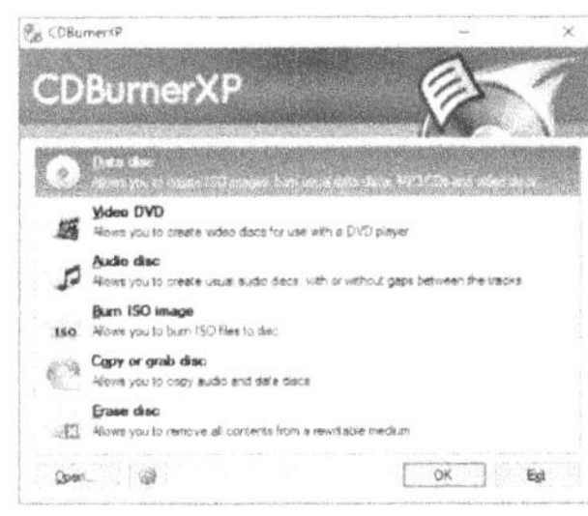
CDBurnerXP
Video DVD
Allows you to create video discs for use with a DVD player
Audio disc
Allows you to create usual audio discs, with or without gaps between the tracks
Burn ISO image
Allows you to burn ISO files to disc
Copy or grab disc
Allows you to copy audio and data discs
Erase disc
Allows you to remove all contents from a rewritable medium
OK

DRIVER
ALLXPSOFT.COM

Top Linux OS
ZORIN OS
KALI

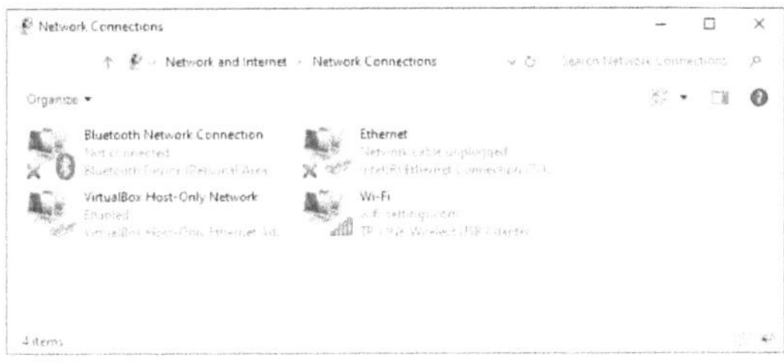
Network Connections
Network and Internet
Network Connections
Organize
Bluetooth Network Connection
Ethernet
VirtualBox Host-Only Network
Wi-Fi

Software Installation

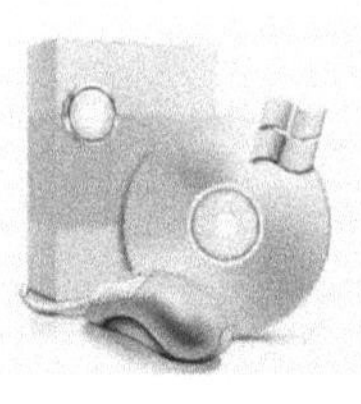

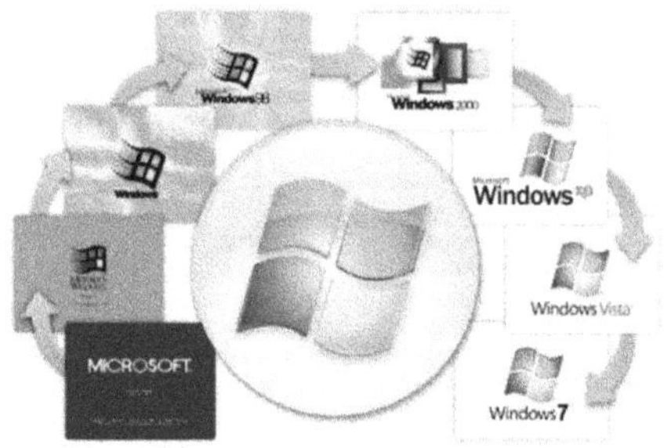

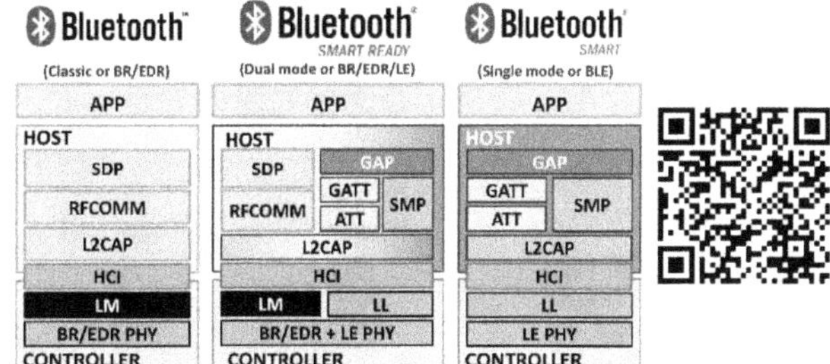

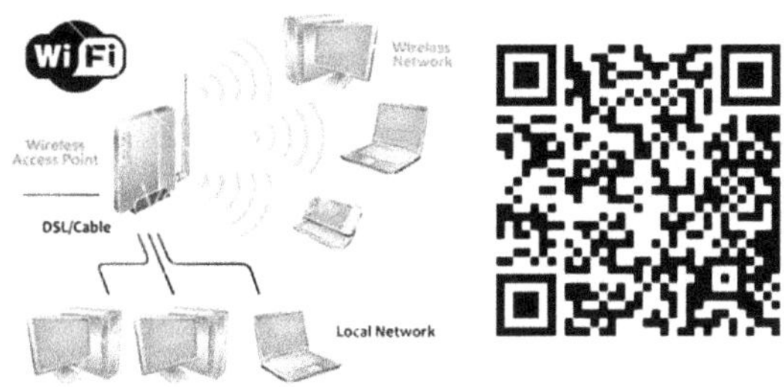

What is a Browser - Definition and

What is
Email?

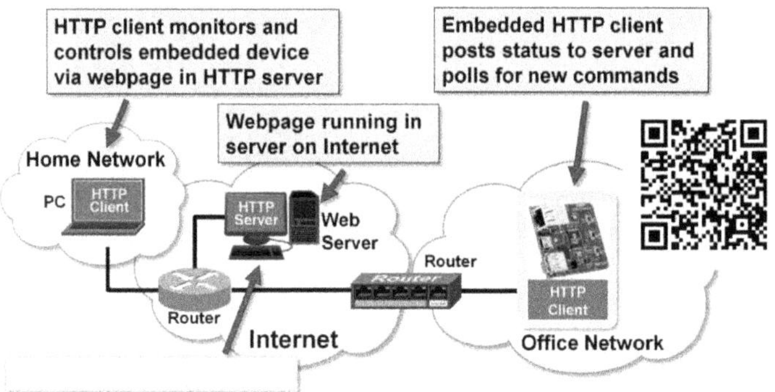
HTTP client monitors and controls embedded device via webpage in HTTP server
Embedded HTTP client posts status to server and polls for new commands
Webpage running in server on Internet
Home Network
PC
HTTP Client
HTTP Server
Web Server
Router
Router
Internet
HTTP Client
Office Network

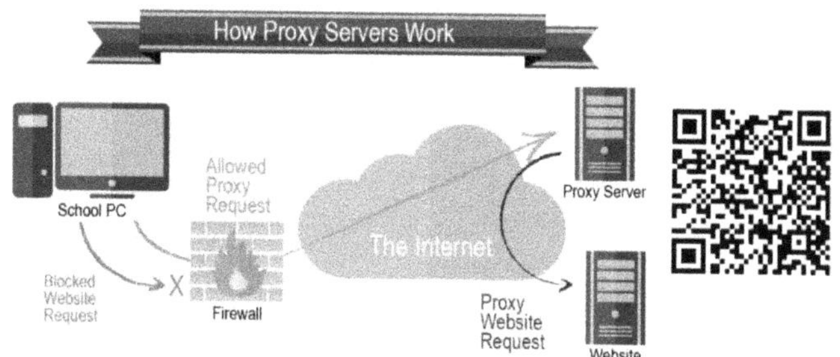
How Proxy Servers Work
School PC
Allowed Proxy Request
Blocked Website Request
Firewall
The Internet
Proxy Server
Proxy Website Request
Website

WWW
What is WWW?

Full HTML & CSS Website
World's Biggest University

Domain-Name-System

Domain-Name-System

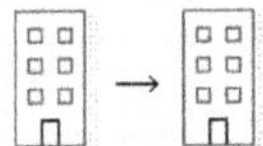

Business to business

Business to consumer

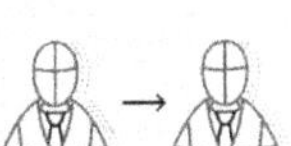

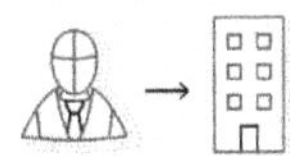

Consumer to consumer

Consumer to business

Payment & Order Processing

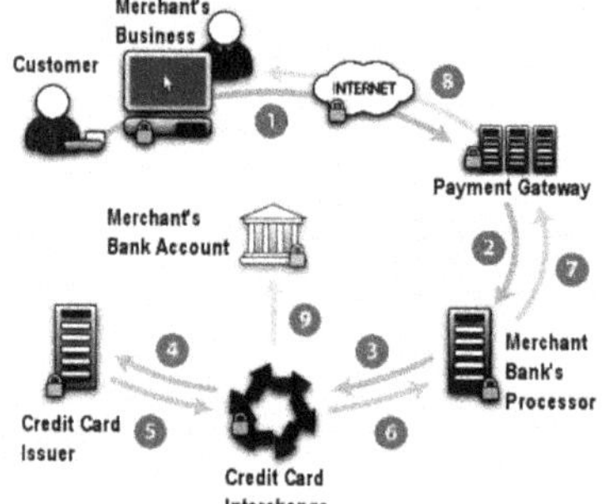

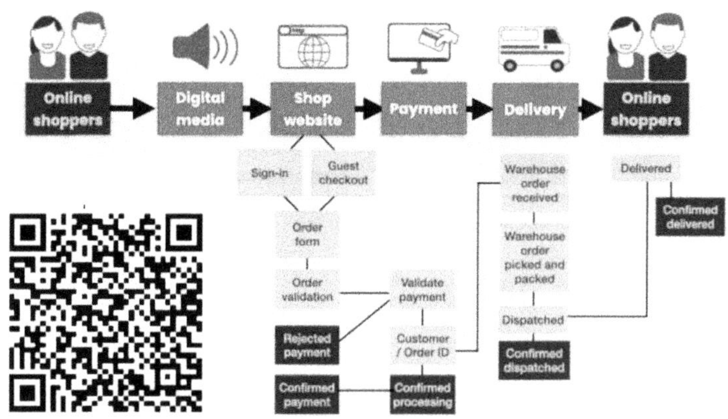
Order to delivery : ideal experience
Online shoppers
Digital media
Shop website
Payment
Delivery
Online shoppers
Sign-in
Guest checkout
Order form
Order validation
Validate payment
Rejected payment
Customer / Order ID
Confirmed payment
Confirmed processing
Warehouse order received
Warehouse order picked and packed
Dispatched
Confirmed dispatched
Delivered
Confirmed delivered

Top 8 Best Payment Gateways for Your Online Store
PayPal
Razorpay
stripe
Braintree
authorize net
Paytm
instamojo
CC Avenue
PAYMENTS
$200

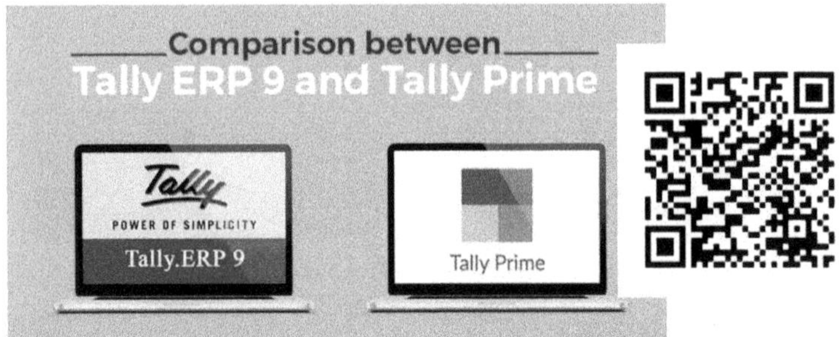
Comparison between
Tally ERP 9 and Tally Prime
Tally
POWER OF SIMPLICITY
Tally.ERP 9
Tally Prime

Social
Networking
Sites
SOCIAL MEDIA
MARKETING

CYBER SECURITY

CHAPTER TWO

English Literacy MCQ

Scan for Theory Videos

1] A resume should be ___________

A] short and precise

B] fancy and colourful

C] having long and detailed information

D] having acronyms and abbreviation

Answer= A

2] A written description of duties and responsibilities to be carrieD] out in A] job is called ____________

A] CV

B] job description

C] resume

D] job application

Answer= B

3] A written description of duties and responsibilities to be carrieD] out in A] job is called____________

A] CV

B] resume

C] job description

D] job application

Answer= C

4] After receiving interview call, what is the next step?

A] SenD] application letter

B] Prepare the resume

C] Appear at interview

D] SenD] resume

Answer= C

5] Choose suitable "wh" word for the given sentence_ "____________ animal do you like?"

A] Which

B] Why

C] Where

D] When

Answer= A

6] Choose the correct punctuation mark after the word "Rohan" in the given sentence_ "Rohan DaviD] and Ram are playing hide and seek".

A] Comma (,)

B] Period (_)

C] Slash (/)

D] Hyphen (-)

Answer= A

7] Choose the correct response for the given question. "How have you been"?

A] Very well, And you?

B] Thank you, And you?

C] Same to you

D] On vacation, And you?

Answer= A

8] Choose the correct response of the given question "When diD] the accident happen"?

A] in the hotel

B] during travelling

C] At 10:30 last night

D] On the table

Answer= C

9] Choose the correct tense of the verb. "I ___________musiC] when I was child."

A] learn

B] am learning

C] will learn

D] learnt

Answer= D

10] Curriculum Vitae (CV) is also known as___________

A] resume

B] job description

C] cover letter

D] application letter

Answer= A

11] Curriculum vitae is also known as ____________

A] circular

B] resume

C] job application form

D] leave application

Answer= B

12] Fill in the blank with comparative adjective "Your pencil is___________ than mine".

A] sharp

B] sharper

C] blunt

D] thick

Answer= B

13] Fill in the blank with correct future tense of verB] "We ____________ to the zoo after Breakfast "

A] went
B] are going
C] had gone
D] will go
Answer= D

14] Fill in the blank with correct word "They __________ good friends"
A] is
B] am
C] are
D] was
Answer= C

15] Fill in the blank with present progressive tense of the verB] "The train ___________ through the tunnel"
A] passed
B] is passing
C] had passed
D] was passing
Answer= B

16] Fill in the blank with proper interrogative adjective " ____________ are you going?
A] Who
B] Where
C] Which
D] What
Answer= B

17] Fill in the blank with proper pronoun "I made this cake ____________"
A] myself
B] yourself
C] himself
D] itself
Answer= A

18] Fill in the blank with proper pronoun. "She made this cake ____________"
A] itself
B] myself
C] herself
D] himself

Answer= C

19] Fill in the blank with proper reflexive pronoun. "She has hurt___________"

A] myself

B] herself

C] himself

D] itself

Answer= B

20] Fill in the blank with suitable adjective for the given sentence "The little girl's...... eyes revealeD] her mischief"

A] chubby

B] weak

C] short sighteD]

D] twinkling

Answer= D

21] Fill in the blank with suitable place preposition_ "My house is ___________the thirD] floor" ?

A] at

B] in

C] on

D] under

Answer= C

22] Fill in the correct question word ______________ is the speaker at the function" ?

A] What

B] When

C] Why

D] Who

Answer= D

23] Low level language is also called ___________

A] source code

B] middle ware

C] machine language

D] assembly language

Answer= C

24] Pronunciation refers to___________

A] diphthong

B] consonant

C] punctuation

D] production of sounD]

Answer= D

25] Re-arrange the following set of words into meaningful sentence_ “teacher / school / worked / she / A] / as”

A] School worked as A she teacher

B] She worked as A school teacher

C] She teacher worked as A school

D] Worked she as A school teacher

Answer= B

26] The word that expresses A sudden and strong feeling is called__________

A] punctuation

B] interjection

C] conjunction

D] apostrophe

Answer= B

27] When you greet higher official’s such as Teacher, Instructor or Supervisor, you should use ____________

A] “Good morning”

B] “Hello”

C] “Hey”

D] “Hi”

Answer= A

28] Which is A silent letter in the word “ANSWER”?

A] R

B] E

C] S

D] W

Answer= D

29] Which one is A “Do’s” of discussion etiquettes?

A] Loose your temper

B] Listen to others

C] Talk about irrelevant details

D] Use impolite or rude language

Answer= B

30] Which one is A “Don’t” of discussion etiquette?

A] Be open mindeD

B] Use moderate tone

C] Listen to others

D] Argue unnecessary

Answer= D

31] Which one is A brain of computer?

A] KeyboarD

B] CPU

C] Monitor

D] HarD disk

Answer= B

32] Which one is A cardinal number?

A] 10

B] V

C] VII

D] XI

Answer= A

33] Which one is A cardinal number?

A] X

B] II

C] IV

D] 3

Answer= D

34] Which one is A cardinal number?

A] IV

B] 10th

C] 1st

D] 1

Answer= D

35] Which one is A cardinal number?

A] One

B] Fifth

C] Eighth

D] SeconD]

Answer= A

36] Which one is an exclamatory sentence?

A] What A beautiful house it is!

B] It is A beautiful house_

C] Is it A beautiful house?

D] Your house is beautiful_

Answer= A

37] Which one is in active voice?

A] Ram has passed the exam_

B] The ball was caught by him_

C] The book was being reaD] by her_

D] We were driven home by dad_

Answer= A

38] Which one is in passive voice?

A] Mohan is painting A house

B] She was reading A book

C] Her birthday was celebrateD by us

D] I have seen that movie

Answer= C

39] Which one is NOT A conjunction?

A] And

B] Or

C] But

D] On

Answer= D

40] Which one is NOT A benefit of the role playing?

A] Builds confidence

B] Develops listening skill

C] Develops creative problem-solving skill

D] Develops boredom

Answer= D

41] Which one is NOT A vowel?

A] A]

B] e

C] f

D] i

Answer= C

42] Which one of the following is A good office etiquette?

A] One should dress formally

B] One should not be punctual to work

C] One should have fancy mobile ring tone

D] One should litter one's work place

Answer= A

43] Word that is pronounceD the same as another word but differs in meaning is called____________________

A] homophone

B] homograph

C] diphthong

D] syllable

Answer= A

CHAPTER THREE

Entrepreneurship skills MCQ

Scan for Theory Videos

1] A person who is associateD with the starting of business is called................

A] merchant

B] entrepreneur

C] businessman

D] sales executive

Answer= B

2] As compareD to small scale business, large scale business require......................

A] less no. of persons

B] less no. of capital

C] more no. of person

D] small machines and tools

Answer= C

3] Entrepreneurship is also termeD as.....

A] investor

B] employer

C] self employment

D] employment seeker

Answer= C

4] For medium manufacturing enterprises, the investment in plant and machinery is between....

A] 10 Lakhs to 2 Crores

B] 25 Lakhs to 5 Crores

C] 2 Crores to 5 Crores

D] 5 Crores to 10 Crores

Answer= D

5] In “SWOT” analysis, “S” stands for..............

A] Success

B] Strength

C] Survey

D] Service

Answer= B

6] In an economiC growth, role of entrepreneur is to.............

A] generate unemployment

B] stagnate standarD of living

C] improve per capitA income

D] unbalance the regional development

Answer= C

7] In SWOT analysis which pair is helpful?

A] Strengths, Weakness

B] Strengths, Opportunities

C] Threats, Weakness

D] Threats, Opportunities

Answer= B

8] Money investeD in purchasing of raw materials, payment of wages and salaries, rental, electricity etC] comes under...........

A] working capital

B] fixeD] capital

C] long term capital

D] capital income

Answer= A

9] MSME stands for..............

A] Micro, Scale and Medium Enterprises

B] Macro, Small and Medium Enterprises

C] Micro, Small and Medium Enterprises

D] Minor, Small and Medium Enterprises

Answer= C

10] PaiD] form of ideas, goods and services are called.............

A] publicity

B] goodwill

C] publiC relation

D] advertisement

Answer= D

11] The enterprises engageD in the production of goods is known as.........

A] manufacturing enterprise

B] service enterprises

C] micro enterprises

D] macro enterprises

Answer= A

12] The expansion of GDP is................

A] Gross DomestiC Product

B] Godown Demand Product

C] Grand Demand Product

D] Giant DomestiC Product

Answer= A

13] The expansion of SIDO is............

A] Small Industries Development Organization

B] Small Income Development Organization

C] Small Investment Development Organization

D] StandarD] Industry Development Organization

Answer= A

14] What approach is useD to gain access to foreign markets and quickly promote an organizations interest?

A] Licensing

B] Collaboration

C] Joint venture

D] Technology transfer

Answer= C

15] Which investment is considered for deciding the status of manufacturing enterprises?

A] Working capital

B] Building and land

C] Plant and machinery

D] Salary of employees

Answer= C

16] Which one is A correct channel through which marketers can reach customers?

A] Manufacture -> Retailer -> Wholesaler -> Customer

B] Manufacturer -> Customer -> Retailer

C] Manufacturer -> Retailer -> Customer

D] Manufacturer -> Retailer -> Customer -> Wholesaler

Answer= C

17] Which one is A weB baseD accounting

A] software designeD for modern business?

B] BUSY

C] TALLY

D] WINGS

Answer= C

CHAPTER FOUR

Productivity MCQ

Scan for Theory Videos

1] During using ATM, Authentication is provideD by customer by entering................

A] cash

B] IFSC]

C] PIN

D] KYC]

Answer= C

2] Expansion of ATM is........

A] Asynchronous Teller Machine

B] AutomateD Teller Machine

C] AutomateD Time Machine

D] Autonomous Time Machine

Answer= B

3] Low productivity will leaD to ....

A] job security

B] political stability

C] decrease in GDP per capitA

D] increase in GDP per capitA

Answer= C

4] Production is defineD] as A ratio of .....

A] output / input

B] input / output

C] output / skill of workmanship

D] input / skill of workmanship

Answer= A

5] Productivity is defineD as the ratio of ....

A] output /input

B] input / output

C] output / skill of the workmanship

D] input / skill of the workmanship

Answer= A

6] The expansion of ATM is ....

A] AutomateD] Tune Machine

B] AutomateD] Teller Machine

C] Asynchronous Teller Machine

D] Asynchronous Time Machine

Answer= B

7] the process useD] by A business to verify the identity of their client is......

A] GDP

B] KYC

C] ATM

D] TFP

Answer= B

8 What is the advantage of automation?

A] ReduceD] operation time

B] High initial cost

C] Unpredictable development cost

D] Security threats

Answer= A

9 What is the unemployment rate if there are 125 million people in the labor force, 100 million people employeD and 25 million are not?

A] 25%

B] 20%

C] 17%

D] 15%

Answer= B

10 Which market determines the real wages and employment?

A] Capital market

B] Labour market

C] Money market

D] Goods market

Answer= B

11 Which one is useD to measure the economiC performance of A whole country or region?

A] KYC]

B] GDP

C] TFP

D] ATM

Answer= B

12 Which one of the following is NOT A category of pure risk?

A] Property risk

B] Technology risk

C] Liability risk

D] Personnel risk

Answer= B

13 Which one of the following is NOT an objective of incentive?

A] ImproveD quality

B] High cost of production

C] High output

D] ReduceD waste

Answer= B

14 Which one of these documents is NOT acceptable for fulfilment of KYC] norms?

A] Voter ID] carD

B] Ration carD

C] Residential certificate

D] Income certificate

Answer= D

15 Which stage is A Period of rapiD revenue growth?

A] Growth stage

B] Maturity stage

C] Decline stage

D] Introduction stage

Answer= A

CHAPTER FIVE

Occupational safety MCQ

Scan for Theory Videos

1 ABC] of first aiD stands for __________________

A] Airway, Bleeding and Circulation

B] Airway, Breathing and Circulation

C] Airway, Bleeding and Compression

D] Airway, Breathing and Compression

Answer= B

2 At what decibels, sounD becomes hazardous noise pollution?

A] Above 30

B] Above 80

C] Above 100

D] Above 120

Answer= B

3 Earthquake is measured with an instrument called ___________

A] telegraph

B] seismograph

C] oscillograph

D] bar graph

Answer= B

4 HeaD] protection is done through ___________

A] helmet

B] goggles

C] gloves

D] mask

Answer= A

5 In firefighting methoD] 'Starvation' is _________

A] limitation of oxygen

B] pouring water

C] elimination of fuel

D] reduction of temperature

Answer= C

6 On the job injuries and illness, cost money time & effort. What is the most practical way to manage these losses?

A] Make sure safety is part of labor contracts

B] Aggressive claims handling

C] Good insurance coverage

D] Effective safety and loss control program

Answer= D

7 Ozone layer is made up of ___________

A] one oxygen atom

B] two oxygen atoms

C] three oxygen atoms

D] four oxygen atoms

Answer= C

8 The reprocessing of discarded materials into new useful products is called _________

A] reuse of waste material

B] recycling of material

C] management of soliD waste

D] reduction in use of raw material

Answer= B

9 The study of living things in relation to their environment is called ....

A] ecosystem

B] economics

C] ecology

D] eclogue

Answer= C

10 The three R's to save environment are ....

A] Reserve, Reduce, Recycle

B] Reuse, Reserve, Reduce

C] Reserve, Reuse, Reduce

D] Reduce, Recycle, Reuse

Answer= D

11 Vibration and radiation comes under ________

A] chemical hazards

B] physical hazards

C] electrical hazards

D] psychological hazards

Answer= B

12 Which one is A man induceD hazards?

A] Landslide

B] Cyclone

C] Volcano

D] Earth quake

Answer= A

13 Which one is A] non-renewable energy resource?

A] Solar

B] Coal

C] Methane

D] HydroelectriC

Answer= B

14 which one is an unsafe condition for work?

A] Oily floor

B] Good light

C] Proper tools

D] Adequate ventilation

Answer= A

15 which one is an unsafe condition for work?

A] Good light

B] Proper tools

C] Adequate ventilation

D] Which factor is NOT concerneD with occupational health and safety?

Answer= A

16 Which one is the main greenhouse gas responsible for global warming?

A] Hydrogen

B] Oxygen

C] Nitrogen

D] Carbon dioxide

Answer= D

17 Which one of the following is NOT an ergonomiC hazard?

A] AwkwarD position

B] Poor housekeeping

C] Emotional disturbances

D] Wrong layout of machinery

Answer= C

18 Which one of the following is not part of 3 R's?

A] Reduce

B] Recycle

C] Regenerate

D] Reuse

Answer= C

CHAPTER SIX

Labour welfare legislation MCQ

Scan for Theory Videos

1 As per factories act, 1948 canteen should be provideD in the factory if, workers are more than..............

A] 100

B] 250

C] 500

D] 1000

Answer= B

2 Under factories Act, the restriction on working time of women is......................

A] before 5 AM and beyonD 7 PM

B] before 6 AM and beyonD 7 PM

C] before 6 AM and beyonD 8 PM

D] before 7 AM and beyonD 8 PM

Answer= B

3 Under Factories Act, the workers weekly hours should not exceeD more than...............

A] 60 hours

B] 50 hours

C] 48 hours

D] 40 hours

Answer= C

4 What is the expansion of ILO?

A] International Labour Organization

B] Indian Labour Organization

C] Indian Labour Occupation

D] International Labour Occupation

Answer= A

5 What is the minimum percentage of employee's contribution from the basiC] salary, as per EPF Act, 1962?

A] 8.50%

B] 9%

C] 12%

D] 12.50%

Answer= C

6 Which amount does include in "wages" amount as per payment wages Act?

A] Dearness allowance

B] Any travelling allowances

C] Any remuneration payable in respect of overtime

D] Any remuneration payable under any awarD

Answer= A

7 Which factor is NOT concerneD with occupational health and safety?

A] Safety

B] Health

C] Welfare

D] Salary

Answer= D

8 Which one of the following is an air pollutant?

A] Oxygen

B] Nitrogen

C] Carbon dioxide

D] Carbon monoxide

Answer= D

9 Which scheme of Act provides health insurance requirements for workers?

A] Factories Act

B] Plantation Labor Act

C] Employee's Compensation Act

D] Employee's state Insurance Act

Answer= D

CHAPTER SEVEN

Quality tools MCQ

Scan for Theory Videos

1 Fishbone chart is also called as.............

A] cause and effect diagram

B] scatter diagram

C] control chart

D] histogram

Answer= A

2 In PDCA cycle, 'P' stands for ....

A] Process

B] Plan

C] Problem

D] Procedure

Answer= B

3 The expansion of QMS is.........................

A] Quality Management StandarD

B] Quality Measurement StandarD

C] Quality Measurement System

D] Quality Management System

Answer= D

4 The PDCA] means...............

A] Plan, Develop, Control, Act

B] Plan, Do, Check, Act

C] Plan, Develop, Check, Act

D] Plan, Do, Control,

Act Answer= B

5 Total number of popular quality tools are....

A] 9

B] 8

C] 7

D] 6

Answer= C

6 What does "SERI" stand for?

A] Sorting out

B] Self-discipline

C] Standardization

D] SystematiC arrangement

Answer= A

7 What is the function of “Histogram” in Quality tools?

A] Narrow down the problem areA

B] Effect of discrete causes

C] Indicates shape of distribution

D] Assess factors for problem

Answer= C

8 What is the last step in ISO 9001 registration?

A] Corrective and preventive action

B] Internal audit

C] Management review meeting

D] Certification and audit

Answer= D

9 What is the name useD for word "waste"?

A] MUDA]

B] MURA]

C] MURI

D] MUSA]

Answer= A

10 Which formulA is correct to quantify the quality

A] Q = P/Q

B] Q = Q/E

C] E = E/P

D] P = Q/P

Answer= A

11 Which one is NOT A basiC tool useD in quality circle?

A] Histogram

B] Pareto chart

C] Check sheet

D] Torque wrench

Answer= D

12 Which one is NOT the certifieD ISO standard?

A] ISO 9010

B] ISO 9001

C] ISO 9002

D] ISO 9003

Answer= A

13 Which one of the following is not the characteristics of quality?

A] Quality control

B] Quality of design

C] Quality of assurance

D] Quality of non- conformance

Answer= D

14 Which statement of quality was stated by quality guru Dr. J. M. Juran?

A] Quality should be aimeD

B] Quality is fitness for use

C] Quality is value for money

D] Quality is conformance to requirement

Answer= B

CHAPTER EIGHT

I.T. Literacy MCQ

Q.1. Which of the following is the biggest unit of memory?
A] Gigabytes.
B] bytes.
C] Megabytes.
D] Kilobytes.
Q.2. The primary purpose of software is to turn data into.
A] Website.
B] Infromation.
C] Programs.

D] Objects.

Q.3. GUI Stands for

A] Graphical User Interface.

B] Greater User Interface.

C] Graphical Union Interface.

D] Graphical User Intereat.

Q.4. Key board keys that have arrows on them are called -

A] Function Keys.

B] Navigation Keys.

C] Typewriter Keys.

D] Special purpose keys.

Q.5. ASSCII, EBCDIC and Unicode are examples of Application Software's

A] True.

B] False.

Q.6. The easiest way to access any part of the screen in the windows operating system is using the.

A] Key Board.

B] Rat.

C] Mouse.

D]] Joystick.

Q.7. A software is also called as a

A] Procedure.

B] Data.

C] Programs.

D] Information.

Q.8. Back programs make copies of the files to be used in case the original files are damaged or lost.

A] True.

B] False.

Q.9. Microprocessor is often called as CPU

A] True.

B] False.

Q.10. .... Utility identifies unnecessary files on the hard disk and erases them based on users command.

A] Backup.

B] File Compression.

C] Uninstall Programs.

D]] Disk Clean up.

Q.11. This type of software is designs to help you be more productive tasks, and is widely used in nearly every disc live and occupation.

A] Communication Software.

B] Utility Software.

C] Basic Application Software.

D] System Software.

Q.12. Minicomputers are also known as.

A] Mid Range Computers.

B] Personal Digital Computers.

C] Mainframe Computers.

D] Laptop Computers.

Q.13. Which of the following device is used to play fast games on a computers.

A] Touch Surface.

B] Touch Screen.2

C] Track Ball.

D] Joystick.

Q.14. Which of the following would not be considered as portable computer.

A] Desktop Computer.

B] Note book computer.

C] Personal Digital Assistant.

D] None of these.

Q.15. Headphone is a typical output device.

A] True.

B] False.

Q.16. Uninstall programs help us to remove unwanted programs installed in the computer.

A] True.

B] False.

Q.17. The capacity of a storage device is usually measured in terms of bytes.

A] True.

B] False.

Q.18. Capacity of the storage device is usually measured in terms of meter.

A] True.

B] False.

Q.19............. is a pointing device.

A] Mouse.

B] Printer.

C] Scanner.

D] Keyboard.

Q.20. The keyboards keys that are labelled F1, F2 and so on are called ....

A] Function Keys.

B] Numeric Keys.

C] Typewriter Keys.

D] Special purpose keys.

Q.21. The keyboard keys like Caps lock that turn on features on or off are called.

A] Function Keys.

B] Combination Keys.

C] Toggle Keys.

D] Special Purpose Keys.

Q.22. Word processing, electronic spread sheets, database managers and graphics programs are all grouped under the title.

A] Browsings Programs.

B] Operating System.

C] Application Software.

D] Data and Information.

Q.23. Keyboard, mouse, monitor, and system unit collectively also known as

A] Solid ware.

B] Software.

C] Hardware.

D] Firm ware.

Q.24. Output of an image on the monitor screen is often called soft copy.

A] True.

B] False.

Q.25. each 0 and 1 in the binary numbering system is called a bit.

A] True.

B] False.

Q.26. Catch memory is used to store most frequently accessed information from the RAM.

A] True.

B] False.

Q.27. The system board is also known as the main board or mother board.

A] True.

B] False.

Q.28. ASSCII, EBCDIC and Unicode are binary coding schemes.

A] True.

B] False.

Q.29. The keys labelled 0-9 on the keyboard are called.

A] Function Keys.

B] Numeric Keys.

C] Typewriter Keys.

D] Special purpose keys.

Q.30. A CD ROM stands for Compact Disk Read Only Memory.

A] True.

B] False.

Q.31. .... consists of step-by-step introductions that tells the computer how to complete the task.

A] Programs.

B] Hardware.

C] Data.

D] Objects.

Q.32. A CD-R stands for CD-Recordable.

A] True.

B] False.

Q.33.......... is a background soft ware that helps the computer to manage its internal resources.

A] System Software.

B] Information.

C] Objects.

D] None of these.

Q.34. Output of an image obtained using a printer is called as hard copy.

A] True.

B] False.

Q.35. Following are the file compression programs, EXCEPT

A] Win Zip.

B] RAID.

C] Win RAR.

D] PK Zip.

Q.36. A track on a disk is one of the many circular ring areas where data is written magnetically.

A] True.

B] False.

Q.37. Floppy disks are removable storage media.

A] True.

B] False.

Q.38. The keyboard keys that have arrows on them are called.

A] Function Keys.

B] Combination Keys.

C] Navigation Keys

D] Special Purpose Keys.

Q.39. Microprocessor is often called as CPU.

A] True.

B] False.

Q.40. Eight bits make up a bite.

A] True.

B] False.

Q.41. Output of an image on the monitor screen is often called hard copy.

A] True.

B] False.

Q.42.......... are graphical objects used to represent and open commonly used applications.

A] G.U.I..

B] Primers'.

C] Windows NT.

D] Icons.

Q.43. A CD-ROM means CD-RW.

A] True.

B] False.

Q.44. Data stored in RAM is

A] Is non-volatile.

B] Is only there while the power is on.

C] Remains only a few minutes after the power is turned off.

D] Is permanent and only lost in power failure.

Q.45. A CD-R stands for CD-Regional.

A] True.

B] False.

Q.46. Primary function of a monitor is to display information to the user.

A] True.

B] False.

Q.47. Random Access Memory] RAM. is .... type of memory.

A] Permanent.

B] Temporary.

C] Flash.

D] Smart.

Q.48 The external memory of the computer is present on the motherboard in the form of slots.

A] False.

B] True.

Q.49 The internal memory of the computer is present on the motherboard in the form of chips

A] True.

B] False.

Q.50 cache memory is used to store most frequently accessed information from the ram.

A] True.

B] False.

Q.1. The "System Date" and "System Time" are the date and time as maintained by the computer's internal clock.

A] True

B] False

Q.2. Disk cleanup is used to rearrange your files so that they are not broken up.

A] True

B] False

Q.3. In Window Vista a folder system is also called a "Directory System."

A] True

B] False

Q.4. "rtf" stands for "rich text format"

A] True

B] False

Q.5. You can click on.............. to learn how to use Windows Vista, obtain troubleshooting information, receive support and more.

A] "Search"

B] "Windows"

C] "Start"

D] "Help & Support"

Q.6. In MS paint to draw a curved line, we have to click the.................... Icon.

A] "Curve"

B] "Line"

C] "Polygon"

D] "Rectangle"

Q.7. .... refers to the height and width of the characters to be printed.

A] "Font Size"

B] "Border"

C] "Cell"

D] "Font Style"

Q.8. There is button which is not present on the "Title bar".

A] Minimize

B] Start

C] Maximise

D] Close

Q.9. Disk Defragmenter is used to remove unnecessary files on your hard disk to free up space and your computer run faster.

A] True

B] False

Q.10. To change the size of your picture, Select "Image Attributes" from the menu.

A] True

B] False

Q.11. To start the calculator application click "Start" and select "All Programs Accessories Calculator."

A] True

B] False

Q.12. .... can be used to create and format large and complex text documents.

A] "Calculator"

B] "WordPad"

C] "Notepad"

D] "Text Pad"

Q.13. Notepad is a basic text editor that can be used to create simple documents.

A] True

B] False

Q.14. A folder system is also called a "................"

A] "Direction System"

B] "Directory System"

C] "Directory list"

D] "Folder book"

Q.15. A folder within a folder is known as a "Folder list."

A] True

B] False

Q.17. A .... is like a container in which you can store files.

A] "Icon"

B] "document"

C] "Folder"

D] "Sheet"

Q.18. The operating system's job is .... to

A] Execute many useful commands easily.

B] to make request for service through a defined application programme interface.

C] to control the computer at the most fundamental level.

D] None of these.

Q.19. The windows interface is based on ....

A] "Graphical user Interface" or GUI

B] Application Programme Interface or] API.

C] "Clipboard"

D] None of these

Q.20. The name of a file consists of two parts, the File Name and the sub file name.

A] True

B] False

Q.21. To access the location of the particular file quickly, you create a shortcut icon for the file and place it on the desktop.

A] True

B] False

Q.22. In Windows Vista windows sidebar contains mini-programs called gadgets.

A] True

B] False

Q.23. A file created using Notepad is stored with the extension..................

A] ".txt"

B] ".docx"

C] ".png"

D] ".jpg"

Q.24. In windows vista two types of "searchers" are supported: Regular search Instant search.

A] True

B] False

Q.25. When your computer is booted and is ready to use, the screen you see is called the ....

A] "Table top"

B] "Desktop"

C] "Laptop"

D] None of these

Q.26. "Computer" is an application which performs functions same as that of a handheld calculator.

A] True

B] False

Q.27. .... is designed to prevent and remove spy ware.

A] User Account Control

B] Windows Firewall

C] Windows Defender

D] Parental Controls

Q.28. The clipboard is not available in Windows Vista Programs.

A] True

B] False

Q.29. What is "Windows Aero"

A] It is the graphical user interface for Windows XP.

B] It is the graphical user interface for Windows Vista.

C] Application Program

D] None of these

Q.30. Which is the basic program of a computer?

A] Operating System

B] Software Program

C] Application Program

D] None of these

Q.31. As you type, the text automatically moves to the next line it reaches the right end of the margin. This feature is called "Word Wrap."

A] True

B] False

Q.32. "Log Off" is a power-saving state.

A] True

B] False

Q.33. In windows vista, you can see multiple programs running simultaneously on different areas of your screen.

A] True

B] False

Q.34. The .... Menu is used to enhance the appearance of the contained presented in a document.

A] "Insert"

B] "Edit" ?

C] "Format"

D] "File"

Q.35. The "text" tool is used to add text to a paint object.

A] True

B] False

Q.36. "............." helps in guarding your computer against malicious software.

A] "Windows Firewall"

B] "Windows Defender"

C] "Spy ware"

D] of these.

Q.37. .... is a basic text editing programme and it is most commonly used to view or edit text files.

A] "Calculator"

B] "Notepad"

C] "Address book"

D] "Paint"

Q.38. In a windows operating system screen saver

A] is helps in guarding your computer against many types of malicious software.

B] is a long, vertical bar that is displayed on the side of your desktop.

C] is a programme that displays on image, animation, or just a blank screen on a Computer after on input has been received for a certain length of time.

D] None of these.

Q.39. Features in Windows Vista make it easier, safer and more entertaining to use your PC virtually anytime and anywhere.

A] True

B] False

Q.40. The programmes on the .... in Windows Vista remain there and are always available for you to click to start them.

A] the "Most frequently use programmes list.

B] "pinned items list"

C] "Documents"

D] "Control Panel"

Q.41. In Windows Vista .... is a power-saving state.

A] Log off

B] Sleep

C] Restart

D] Lock

Q.42. AERO is an abbreviation of ....

A] Authentic, Energetic, Reflective and Open.

B] Essential, Reflective and Open.

C] Arithmetic, Essential, Reflective and Object.

D] Authentic, Essential, Reflective and Open.

Q.43. At the bottom of the screen, you can see a long, thin bar which is called as ....

A] "Task bar"

B] "Title bar"

C] "Menu bar"

D] "Spacebar"

Q.44. In Windows Vista a "Clipboard" is ....

A] an application program

B] a temporary storage area for information that you have copied or moved from one place and plan to use somewhere else.

C] an operating system.

D] None of these.

Q.45. .... is a basic text editing programme and it is most commonly used to view or edit text files.

A] "Calculator"

B] <u>"Notepad"</u>

C] "Address book"

D] "Paint"

Q.46. ...., is a drawing programme that can be used to create modify graphic images.

A] "Brush"

B] <u>"Paint"</u>

C] "Notepad"

D] "WordPad"

Q.47. The .... menu is used to enhance the apperance of the content presented in a document.

A] "Insert"

B] "Edit"

C] <u>"Format"</u>

D] "File"

Q.48. A .... is a rectangular section on the screen that is used to display information and other programme.

A] Icon

B] Desktop

C] <u>Window</u>

D] Panel

Q.49. The capability of an operating system to run multiple programmes at the same time is called "Multitasking."

A] <u>True</u>

B] False

Q.50. In Window vista, you can see multiple Programme running simultaneously on different areas of your screen

A]<u>True</u>

B] False

Q.51. The name of a file consist of two parts

A] Folder Name

B] use Extension

C] <u>File Name</u>

D] use Sub folder Name

Q.52. We can navigate through text using

A] Cpu

B] Mouse

C] Key board

D] Monitor

Q.1. In MS Word 2007 when text is selected, a "............" is automatically displayed.

A] Taskbar

B] Main Toolbar

C] Mini Toolbar

D] Menu bar

Q.2. You can make for a TOC using:

A] Heading styles.

B] Custom styles.

C] Outline levels.

D] All of these.

Q.3. .... contains command for opening, saving, printing and closing a file.

A] "Home"

B] "Office Button"

C] "View"

D] "Insert"

Q.4. .... offers a wide variety of options to design documents.

A] Microsoft Excel

B] Microsoft PowerPoint

C] Microsoft Word

D] Microsoft Access

Q.5. All of the following Ribbon tabs are displayed in Word 2007, EXCEPT

A] Home

B] Insert

C] Tools

D] Page Layout

Q.6. When you use the mouse to move the insertion point, the shape of mouse pointer is like I-beam.

A] True

B] False

Q.7. Index shows you at a glance, the topics that are included in the document and make it easier to locate information.

A] True

B] False

Q.8. You can click on the "Format" tab under "WordArt tools" to modify the WordArt as per your requirements.

A] True

B] False

Q.9. In Word, a file is called as a ....

A] "template"

B] "form"

C] "database"

D] "Document"

Q.10. The Mail Marge feature, combines a list of data, typically a file of names and addresses.

A]True

B] False

Q.11. Microsoft Word is the only word processor available in the market.

A] True

B] False

Q.12. Hyperlink identifies a location in the document or a section of text that you name for feature reference.

A] True

B] False

Q.13. A .... is a reference from one part of a document to related information in same another part.

A] Hyperlink

B] Cross-reference

C] Document

D] Linkage

Q.14. For Indentation you may use the "Decrease Indent" and "Increase Indent" icons in the "Paragraph" group on the "............" tab for indenting your text.

A] Insert

B] Home

C] Page Layout

D] Data

Q.15. In MS Word 2007 the "References" tab contains spell check, the squares, and track changes.

A] True

A] False

Q.16. The "..............." is a dictionary of synonyms which you can use to find words that are synonyms with a term.

A] Translate

B] Spelling

C] Thesaurus

D] Research

Q.17. A " .... " is a listing of the topics that appear in a document with their associated page references.

A] Index

B] Table

C] Clipboard

D] Table of contents

Q.18. You can format your document automatically applying styles, available in MS Word 2007.

A] True

B] False

Q.19. A "............" is a connection to a location in the current document to another document or Web Site.

A] Link

B] hyperlink

C] hypolink

D] linkage

Q.20. To view a document in the Print Preview Mode, click on the Office Button and select "Print Print Preview."

A] True

B] False

Q.21. You may use the "The Auto Complete Feature" to automatically correct the grammatical and spelling mistakes in your document.

A] True

B] False

Q.22. Using a word Processing application you can create, modify, store, retrieve and print a document.

A] True

B] False

Q.23. "Mini Toolbar" provides easy way to access the most frequently used formatting commands.

A] True

B] False

Q.24. To print only selected pages in your documnet, you may use either the "Current page" or "Page" option under "Print Range."

A] True

B] False

Q.25. MS Word 2007 when we click on the Office Button the "Edit" menu is displayed.

A] True

B] False

Q.26. A "................." is a pre-designed document useful for creating common purpose documents such as a fax, invoice or business letter.

A] Template

B] File

C] Form

D] Database

Q.27. A multileve list shows the list items at different levels rather then single level.

A] True

B] False

Q.28. A "............" is used to organize information into an easy-to-read format of horizontal rows and vertical columns.

A] Cell

B] Sheet

C] Box

D] Table

Q.29. To remove individual character at the left you may press "............".

A] Delete

B] Backspace

C] Enter

D] Spacebar

Q.30. When you click on "Format Printer" icon on the "Home" tab, you can see that your mouse pointer changes to a "............" icon.

A] paintbrush

B] I-beam

C] Arrow

D] 4-Way arrow

Q.31. You may create a new document using standard templates provided by Word by checking on a template name in the "New Document" window.

A] True

B] False

Q.32. MS Word's Mail Merge feature facilitates you to mail your document about special offers to a large number of people.

A] True

B] False

Q.33. When you move your mouse over a button, a .... is displayed. That provides a detailed description of what the button does.

A] Super-tooltip

B] Sub-tooltip

C] Info

D] Key-tip

Q.34. MS Word 2007 can quickly sort text, data or numbers ascending or descending order.

A] True

B] False

Q.35. .... Applications help you to create different types of written documents such as personal letters, from letters, brochures, faxes and even professional manuals.

A] Word Processor

B] Word Pad

C] Note Pad

D] None of these

Q.36. The "Mailings" tab contains the items required for mail merge.

A] True

B] False

Q.37. Word places footnotes at the end of each page and end notes at the end of documents.

A] True

B] False

Q.38. To remove the hyperlink while retaining the text, right - click on it and select "Remove Hyperlink."

A] True

B] False

Q.39. MS Word indicates formatting inconsistencies with a red wavy underline.

A] True

B] False

Q.40. To automatically correct the document, we use

A] The auto correct feature

B] The auto complete feature

C] Formatting

D] Building Blocks

Q.41. A "..............." is a common application for news paper columns.

A] News reading

B] News letter

C] News

D] News editor

Q.42. Personal letters, form letters, brochures, faxes and professional manuals can be using word processors.

A] True

B] False

Q.43. The set margins, select "Margins" from the "Page Setup" group on the "Page Layout" tab.

A] True

B] False

Q.44. Drop caps are the first characters at the beginning of a paragraph that are enlarged, conversing several lines.

A] True

B] False

Q.45. A multilevel list shows the list items at different levels rather than single level.

A] True

B] False

Q.46. The "Page Layout" tab contains margin, orientation, and spacing properties.

A] True

B] False

Q.47. A "............." is used to mark a certain location in a document.

A] Index

B] Hyperlink

C] Bookmark

D] Table

Q.48. You may click on "Replace All" button to replace all occurrences of the search text by specified new text.

A] True

B] False

Q.49. While working on a document in MS Word 2007 when we click on the picture, it is surrounded by eight boxes called "Sizing handles" which is used to to change the size of the graphic.

A] True

B] False

Q.50. While changing the level of an item in hierarchy you can increase the indent by using

A] "Tab"

B] "Backspace"

C] "Delete"

D] "Spacebar"

Q.51. Footnotes or Endnotes are used to provide certain "........................".

A] References

B] Information

C] Points

D] Lists

Q.52. If you want the data to be automatically get updated in a document when the current data changes, check the "Update automatically" box.

A] True

B] False

Q.1. In formula bar, an adjacent range is specified by giving the starting and editing cell addresses separated by a

A] Semicolon

B] Comma

C] Full stop

D] Colon

Q.2. The cell address is displayed in the "Text Box".

A] True

B] False

Q.3. A .... is a visual representation of data and conveys the information in an easy to understand and attractive manner.

A] chart

B] table

C] picture

D] graphic

Q.4. In formulas, a non-adjacent range is specified by giving the cell addresses separated by a ....

A] Semicolon

B] Comma

C] Full stop

D] Colon

Q.5. You can use the .... to enter and edit data, instead of editing directly in your work sheet.

A] formula bar

B] title bar

C] menu bar

D] space bar

Q.6. Your Excel 2007 file is stored with the extension "............".

A] ".docx"

B] ".xlsx"

C] ".xltx"

D] ".zltx"

Q.7. In an electronic spreadsheet or worksheet, data can be edited, new data can be added, and unwnated data can be deleted.

A] True

B] False

Q.8. The "Review" tab contains proofing tools like spell check & also has button that let you add comments to a worksheet and manage revisions.

A] True

B] False

Q.9. The "............" tab contains proofing tools like spell check.

A] "Review"

B] "Data"

C] "View"

D] "Insert"

Q.10. You can create and design our own work book templates.

A] True

B] False

Q.11. In a spreadsheet programme as you move from one cell to another, the reference or address to the active cell appears in the "Name Box."

A] True

B] False

Q.12. To start the Microsoft Excel Application, click on the "Start" button and select "All programmes Microsoft Office ? Microsoft Office Excel 2007.

A] True

B] False

Q.13. The "Insert" tab lets you add special ingredients like tables, graphics, charts, and hyperlinks in a spreadsheets programme.

A] True

B] False

Q.14. The text that appears in the bottom margin of the page is called as the "Footer".

A] True

B] False

Q.15. In Excel, a formula always begins with an equal sign] =. and uses arithmetic operators like +, -, *, /, %, and ^ to perform addition, subtraction, multiplication, division, percent and exponentiation respectively.

A] True

B] False

Q.16. While working you may have to reference data from more than one sheet which is called referencing multiple sheets.

A] True

B] False

Q.17. The defalut page orientation setting is "Landscape".

A] True

B] False

Q.18. "............." is a method which aids you in forecasting values.

A] "Find"

B] "Replace"

C] "Goal Seek"

D] "Go to"

Q.19. In MS Excel 2007, below the "Ribbon", we can see Name Box on the left and the Formula Bar on the right.

A] True

B] False

Q.20. A "..............." is a prewritten formula the performs calculations automatically.

A] "Function"

B] "Equation"

C] "Template"

D] "Reaction"

Q.21. MS Excel 2007 is used for different types of .... varying from vary simple to complex.

A] calculations

B] manipulations

C] presentations

D] expressions

Q.22. Your excel file is stored with the extension ".xltx".

A] True

B] False

Q.23. "Autocorrect" is a feature of Microsoft Excel 2007 that makes entering a series of heading easier by logically repeating and extending the series.

A] True

B] False

Q.24. "A relative reference" is a cell or range reference used in a formula whose location does not change when a formula is copied.

A] True

B] False

Q.25. While changing the level of an item in the hierarchy you can increase the indent by using.

A] "Tab"

B] "Backspace"

C] "Delete"

D] "Spacebar"

Q.26. To set margins, select "Margins" from the "Page Setup" group on the "Page Layout" tab.

A] True

B] False

Q.27. To remove individual character at the left you may press "..............".

A] Delete

B] Backspace

C] Enter

D] Spacebar

Q.28. Drop caps are the first character/s at the beginning that are enlarged, conversing several lines.

A] True

B] False

Q.29. The intersection of a row and a column is called a "................".

A] Table

B] Cell

C] Data

D] Sheet

Q.30. A .... is a file that is provided by the application in a "ready to use" format.

A] Sheet

B] Template

C] Book

D] Report

Q.31. A .... is a visual representation of data and conveys the information in a easy to understand and attractive manner.

A] Chart

B] Table

C] Picture

D] Graphic

Q.32. To move among the worksheet in your workbook, you need to click on the "Workbook" tab.

A] True

B] False

Q.33. A theme comprise of a colour palette, font set, and effects.

A] True

B] False

Q.34. You can view two areas of worksheet and lock rows or columns in one area by splitting or freezing panes.

A] True

B] False

Q.35. "............" are individual designs that can be applied to different parts to the document.

A] "Graphics"

B] "Styles"

C] "Pictures"

D] "Themes"

Q.36. "............" contains commands for opening, saving, printing, and closing a file.

A] "View" tab

B] "Office Button"

C] "Insert" tab

D] "Review" tab

Q.37. When a formula containing an absolute cell reference is copied to another row or column in the worksheet, the cell reference does not change.

A] True

B] False

Q.38. The "header" is usually the title you give on the page.

A] True

B] False

Q.39. The text that appears in the top margin of the page is called the ....

A] Footer

B] Column

C] Header

D] Paragraph

Q.40. In a spreadsheet programme a table is a selection of two or more cells.

A] True

B] False

Q.41. The "title" is usually given as the footer.

A] True

B] False

Q.42. To stop the automatic relative cell references, i.e. to make the cell reference absolute, type a .... character before the column and row number.

A] # hash.

B] $ dollar.

C] % percent.

D] * star.

Q.43. A theme comprise of a colour palette, font set, and effects.

A] True

B] False

Q.44. To select a group or range of cells, click on the cell you want to begin, drag your cursor and release it when you have reached the end of the selection.

A] True

B] False

Q.45. If we require to add more data to be on one page, we change the page orientation to land scape.

A] True

B] False

Q.46. Each worksheet can be used to organized different types of related information.

A] True

B] False

Q.47. The "table" is a visual representation of data and convey the information in an easy to understand and attractive manner.

A] True

B] False

Q.48. "Themes" provided with MS Excel 2007 are universal designs that unify all of the styles.

A] True

B] False

Q.49. In Microsoft Excel 2007, a single file or document is called a ".............".

A] Workbook

B] Worksheet

C] Sheet

D] Notebook

Q.50. "Notebook" contains a collection of one or more worksheets and, optionally, chart sheets containing graphic pictures of your worksheet data.

A] True

B] False

Q.51. With the .... option, you can freeze either or both, rows and columns ie. regardless of where you are in the worksheet you can see the information in these rows and/or columns at all times.

A] Split

B] Arrange

C] Fitter

D] Freeze Panes

Q.52. You can create charts to represent data more effectively in an electronic sheet or worksheet.

A] True

B] False

Q.53. In a spreadsheet each cell has its own address called as "cell address".

A] True

B] False

Q.54. A template file in MS Excel 2007 has an extension "................".

A] .docx

B] .yltx

C] .xltx

D] .zltx

Q.55. A "............" is like an accountant's ledger consisting of rows and columns.

A] Table

B] Microsoft Excel 2007

C] Format

D] Sheet

Q.56. A "table" is a visual representation of data and conveys the information in an easy to understand and attractive manner.

A] True

B] False

Q.1. The "Insert" tab contains the basic set of objects which you can insert into a slide.

A] True

B] False

Q.2. Click "Replace All" to replace all occurrences of search text by the specified new text.

A] True

B] False

Q.3. A "................" graphic is a visual representation of your information and ideas.

A] "WordArt"

B] "ClipArt"

C] "SmartArt"

D] "Autoshape"

Q.4. To start a Microsoft PowerPoint Application, click on the "Start" button and select "All progrmmes ? Microsoft Office ? Microsoft Office PowerPoint 2007".

A] True

B] False

Q.5. "..............." refer to a ready-to-use picture.

A] "WordArt"

B] "ClipArt"

C] "SmartArt"

D] "Autoshape"

Q.6. To open a recently used presentation you may click the office button and then click on the presentation name in the list displayed under "Recent Documents".

A] True

B] False

Q.7. SmartArt programs are designed to help you to create an effective presentation.

A] True

B] False

Q.8. The "............" tab contains tools that controls how to slide show is presented.

A] "Design"

B] "Slide Show"

C] "Review"

D] "View"

Q.9. Minature pictures of slides displayed in the slide sorter view.

A] True

B] False

Q.10. .... which displays icon that represent commonly used commands such as Save, Undo, and Redo.

A] Home Button

B] The Ribbon

C] The Quick Access Tool bar

D] The Office Button

Q.11. A "..........." is a connection to a location in the current documnet, another document or a website.

A] Highlink

B] hipolink

C] linkage

D] hyperlink

Q.12. .... are used to create slide shows on the computer

A] Presentation graphics

B] Analytical development programs

C] Super Slide packages

D] Slide maker tools

Q.13. To preview your presentation as web page, you need to add the "Web Page Preview" command to Ribbon.

A] True

B] False

Q.14. With "Slide Show View" you can see how your graphics timings, movies, animated elements and transition effects will look in the actulashow.

A] True

B] False

Q.15. In graphic presentation, programmes each presentation is divided into ....

A] charts

B] slides

C] tables

D] pictures

Q.16. In PowerPoint "Match case": you may check this box for a case sensitive search.

A] True

B] False

Q.17. "Scale to fit paper": check this box to print the slides with an outer frame.

A] True

B] False

Q.18. In PowerPoint "build effects" are animations to slide contents..

A] True

B] False

Q.19. A "..............." is a pre-designed presentation designed for common purpose such as photo album or a quiz show.

A] "Chart"

B] "Table"

C] "Slide"

D] "Template"

Q.20. You may create a new presentation using a template provided by PowerPoint.

A] True

B] False

Q.21. We can insert a video clip on a PowerPoint Slide.

A] True

B] False

Q.22. When you move your mouse over a sizing handle the pointer becomes a "............".

A] Round Arrow

B] Two-headed Arrow

C] Plus Sign

D] Four-headed Arrow

Q.23. PowerPoint Presentation is a component of following application software.

A] Leap Office

B] Start Office

C] Open Office

D] MS Office

Q.24. "Slide Show View" is an exclusive view of your slides in thumbnail form.

A] True

B] False

Q.25. Headers and Footers are used to add information such as slide numbers, the time and date, a company logo or the presentation title to the top of a hand out or notes page in your presentation, or to bottom of a slide, handout or notes page.

A] True

B] False

Q.26. To see a preview of your slide in a window on the screen, click on the Quick Access Toolbar and select "Print ? Print Preview".

A] True

B] False

Q.27. In Graphics Presentation Programs each presentation is divided into charts.

A] True

B] False

Q.28. Using WordArt graphics, you can effectively communicate your message in a quick and msimple way.

A] True

B] False

Q.29. You may change the presentation views by checking on the buttons displayed on the "..........." at the bottom of the screen.

A] "Title bar"

B] "Menu bar"

C] "Tool bar"

D] "Status bar"

Q.30. "Animations" refers to addition of special visual or sound effect to your slides.

A] True

B] False

Q.31. Using PowerPoint presentation graphics is simple and it is used for effective presentation

A] on a topic.

B] True

C] False

Q.32. A "review" is a way to looking at a presentation.

A] True

B] False

Q.33. In Presentation Graphics "..........." are used to add information such as slide numbers, the time and date, a company logo or the presentation title to the top of a handout or notes page in your presentation, or a bottom of a slide, handout or notes.

A] Hyperlinks

B] Tables

C] Header and Footers

D] Charts

Q.34. The sizing handles at the slides are used to adjust only the height or the width.

A] True

B] False

Q.35. "..............." takes up the full computer screen, like an actual slide show presentation.

A] Slide Sorter View

B] Normal View

C] Slide Show View

D] Notes Page

Q.36. The "Outline" tab shows your slide text in outline form.

A] True

B] False

Q.37. A slide layout refers to the arrangements of elements, such as text, pictures, tables, charts and movies, on a slide.

A] True

B] False

Q.38. If you have a large number of slides in your presentation, you may find it more convenient to use the .... to view all your slides and change their positions.

A] Normal View

B] Slide Sorter View

C] Slide Show View

D] Notes Page

Q.39. You may use either the Normal View or the Slide Sorter View to delete a Slide.

A] True

B] False

Q.40. In Microsoft PowerPoint your file is stored with the .... extension.

A] psd

B] .rtf

C] .pptx

D] .docx

Q.41. When the pointer becomes a ...., you can drag placeholder to the location you wish.

A] Round arrow

B] Two-round arrow

C] Plus sign

D] Four-headed arrow

Q.42. A "Clip" may be a single media file, including art, sound, animation or movies.

A] True

B] False

Q.43. "............" are details about a file that help identify it.

A] Desktop Properties

B] Window Properties

C] Advanced Properties

D] Document Properties

Q.44. The "Sizing Handles" at the slides and corners of the selection rectangle can be used to adjust the size of the place holder.

A] <u>True</u>

B] False

Q.45. To open a file that you have previously saved, click the Ribbon and select "Open".

A] True

B] <u>False</u>

Q.46. "..............." is the main editing view.

A] Slide Sorter View

B] <u>Normal View</u>

C] Slide Show View

D] Notes Page

Q.47. We can insert a audio clip on a powerpoint slide.

A] <u>True</u>

B] False

Q.48. In PowerPoint the “Insert” tab contains tools to design your slides.

A] True

B] <u>False</u>

Q.49. The “...........” tab contains the basic formatting tools.

A] “Design”

B] “View”

C] “Insert”

D] <u>”Home”</u>

Q.50. The “Slides” tab makes it easy to navigate through your presentation and to see the effects of changes and also rearrange, add or delete sliders.

A] <u>True</u>

B] False

Q.51. The “Outline” tab shows you slides as your thumbnail sized images while you edit.

A] True

B] <u>False</u>

Q.52. In PowerPoint the “Insert” tab contains tools to design your slides.

A] True

B] <u>False</u>

Q.1. You can start the name of the field with a space.

A] True.

B] False.

Q.2. "............" is a database object that is mainly used to enter and display records and make changes to existing records on screens.

A] query.

B] form.

C] report.

D] table.

Q.3. Primary Number is a unique, sequential number that is automatically incremented by one whenever a new record is added to the table.

A] True.

B] False.

Q.4. each column is a record which is the smallest unit of information about a record.

A] True.

B] False.

Q.5. A form is a printed output generated from tables and queries.

A] True.

B] False.

Q.6. The ribbon has Task-oriented Tabs, Groups and command buttons.

A] True.

B] False.

Q.7. "............" is an electronic database management system which can store, organize access, manipulate, and present information in many different ways.

A] MS Access 2007.

B] MS Word.

C] MS Excel.

D] MS PowerPoint.

Q.8. A professional database is the most widely used database structure.

A] True.

B] False.

Q.9. The tables are related or linked to one another by a common field.

A] True.

B] False.

Q.10. When you select a data type, its default properties are displayed under "Display Properties."

A] True.

B] False.

Q.11. ".............." data type is used to store numbers only.

A] Auto Number.

B] Text.

C] Number.

D] Date/Time.

Q.12. A default value is used to specify a value that is automatically entered in a field when a new record is added.

A] True.

B] False.

Q.13. "............" stores the information in Access 2007.

A] Table.

B] Queries.

C] Reports.

D] Forms.

Q.14. A field property is a characteristic that helps to define a field.

A] True.

B] False.

Q.15. ".........." data type is used to store images, documents, graphs etc.

A] Hyperlink.

B] OEL Object.

C] Text.

D] Description.

Q.16. ".........." decides the maximum number of characters that can be entered in the field.

A] Format.

B] Input Mask.

C] Caption.

D] Field Size.

Q.17. The information in a database is stored in a ....

A] Chart.

B] Box.

C] Folder.

D] Table.

Q.18. "............" is the default data type and is used to store text entries like words, combinations of words and numbers and numbers that are not used in calculations.

A] Text.

B] Number.

C] Memo.

D] Currency.

Q.19. In Access, you can sort data in ascending or descending order.

A] True.

B] False.

Q.20. Access provides different window formats called "Lists" to display and work with the objects in a database.

A] True.

B] False.

Q.21. In Access, every database is stored in a single file which has the extension.

A] ".docx"

B] ".rtf"

C] ".accdb"

D] ".txt"

Q.22. The data type defines the type of data the field will contain.

A] True.

B] False.

Q.23. A .... is used to identify the data stored in a field.

A] Table.

B] Field Name.

C] Box.

D] Bracket.

Q.24. A database is an organized collection of related information.

A] True.

B] False.

Q.25. ".........." simplifies data entry and controls what data is required and how it is to be displayed.

A] Format.

B] Input Mask.

C] Caption.

D] Field Size.

Q.26. Access automatically creates a code for the primary key, which helps makes queries and other operations.

A] True.

B] False.

Q.27. .... provides a number of data types.

A] Word 2007.

B] Access 2007.

C] Excel 2007.

D] PowerPoint 2007.

Q.28. It is difficult to add, delete and modify records from a table.

A] True.

B] False.

Q.29. The "Form Wizard" feature of Access 2007 makes it very easy to design forms.

A] True.

B] False.

Q.30. When you open a database or create a new one, the names of your database objects such a tables. Forms and reports appear in the Navigation Pane.

A] True.

B] False.

Q.31. Charts are made up of vertical columns] called fields. and horizontal rows] called records.

A] True.

B] False.

Q.32. You can quickly produce reports using some MS Access features.

A] True.

B] False.

Q.33."..........." are windows that you create and arrange in order to easily view or change the information in a table.

A] Table.

B] Queries.

C] Report.

D] Forms.

Q.34. ".........." restricts the data easy to meet certain conditions or requirements.

A] Validation Text.

B] Default Value.

C] Validation Rule.

D] Format.

Q.35. Forms help you print same or all of the information in a table.

A] True.

B] False.

Q.36. "..........." data type is used to store text that is too long to be stored in a text field.

A] Text.

B] Number.

C] Memo.

D] Currency.

Q.37. The "Description" text box is used to describe the field.

A] True.

B] False.

Q.38. "............" specifies a field caption or a prompt for the user to enter data.

A] Format.

B] Input Mask.

C] Caption.

D] Field Size.

Q.39. "Form Wizard" guides you through the steps required to create a form.

A] True.

B] False.

Q.40. A field name is to identify the data stored in a field.

A] True.

B] False.

Q.41. A default value is an expression that defines acceptable values.

A] True.

B] False.

Q.42. Each row is a field which contains all the information about a person, thing or place.

A] True.

B] False.

Q.43. A primary key must be

A] Unique But Permit Null.

B] Unique and Not Null.

C] Non-unique And Not Null.

D] Non-unique And Permit Null.

Q.44. which of the following are functions performed by a DBA?

A] Database Design.

B] System Security.

C] Backup and Recovery.

D] All of the above.

Q.45. "..........." is a relation database management application that is used to create and analyze a database.

A] Word 2007.

B] Access 2007.

C] System Security.

D] PowerPoint 2007.

Q.46. You can create as many tables as you need to store different types of information.

A] True.

B] False.

Q.47. A "............" is a field or set of fields in your table that provide Access with a unique identifier for every record.

A] Password.

B] Special Code.

C] Primary Key.

D] Unique Code.

Q.48. The photo can be inserted as a file.

A] True.

B] False.

Q.49. You can analyze the data in a table and perform calculations on different fields of data.

A] True.

B] False.

Q.50. Formatting the data often helps in finding some particular information quickly.

A] True.

B] False.

Q.51. what is the first step of defining a database.

A] Designing the database.

B] Collection of data.

C] Planning your database.

D] Digitizing your data.

Q.52. The "Print Preview" tab appears when you view the table in the print preview mode.

A] True.

B] False.

Q.53. Datasheet view can be used to create and view the design of all types of database objects such as tables, forms, queries, and reports.

A] True.

B] False.

Q.54. DBMS means..................

A] Database Management System.

B] Domain Management System.

C] Domain Manangeemt Server.

D] Domain Management Style.

Q.55. Access also ensure that every record has a non-blank primary key field, and that it is always unique.

A] True.

B] False.

Q.56. “Validation Rule” specifies a default value for a field to be automatically field n at the time of data entry.

A] True.

B] False.

Q.57. Design view provides a row and column view of the data in tables, forms, and queries.

A] True.

B] False.

Q.58 You can enter up to charactess in a text field.

A] 375

B] 125

C] 235

D] 255

Q.1. Netscape Navigator is a type of ....

A] Utility Program.

B] Operating System.

C] Browser.

D] Web Authoring Program.

Q.2. When you type an address such as "http://www.mkcl.org", in this .org indicates.

A] Original Web Site.

B] Commercial Web Site.

C] Organizational Web Site.

D] Educational Web Site.

Q.3. You can search the World Wide Web for a specific topic by using ………… and……………..

A] Gophers, Fido's.

B] Scanner, Search Engine.

C] Search Engines, Indexes.

D Browsers, Larkers.

Q.4. A] n. ………… is a set of rules for how information and messages are sent over the internet.

A] Protocol.

B] ISP.

C] Applet.

D] HTML Hyper Text Markup Language.

Q.5. Discussion on the internet about specific topic is known as

A] News.

B] News group.

C] Veronica.

D] Telnet.

Q.6. Which of the following is not a type of protocol?

A] TCI/IP

B] ASCII

C] None of these.

D] ppp

Q.7. Which of the following is a type of protocol?

A] ASCII

B] RAM

C] TCI/IP

D] DBA

Q.8. The three parts of an e-mail message are

A] TCP/IP, Domain and ISP.

B] Destination, Device and Sender.

C] Header, Message and Signature.

D] TCP, IP and Message.

Q.9. The network connecting several computers all over the world is?

A] Intranet.

B] Internet.

C] Arpanet.

D] Network.

Q.10. Which of the following is a browser.

A] Web site.

B] Microsoft.

C] Internet Explorer.

D] www.

Q.11. The terms DNS stands for.

A] Data Naming System.

B] Do Name System.

C] Domain Name System.

D] Duplicate Name System.

Q.12. Internet e-mail address is .... for every user.

A] Unique.

B] Same.

C] Common.

D] None of these.

Q.13. For navigating any website, user has to enter

A] URL.

B] www.

C] PPP.

D] None of these.

Q.14. What is the full form of E-Commerce ?

A] English Commerce.

B] Electronic Commerce.

C] Electric Commerce.

D] Element Commerce.

Q.15. To send e-mail to someone you need ....

A] Resident Address.

B] Internet Connectivity.

C] Fax Address.

D] None of these.

Q.16. .... is used to see the web page.

A] Inbox.

B] Recycle bin.

C] Internet Explorer.

D] Network Neighbourhood.

Q.17. Full form of URL

A] Universal Resource Locator.

B] Uniform Resource Locator.

C] Uni Resource Locator.

D] None of these.

Q.18. Modem converts data from a CD to a hard disk.

A] True.

B] False.

Q.19. Which of the following is a search engine.

A] Google.

B] Alta Vista.

C] Yahoo.

D] All of these.

Q.20. What is meant by E-Commerce?

A] Online selling, purchasing, account handling etc.

B] Subject commerce stream.

C] Electronic equipment to deal with commercial problem.

D] All of the above.

Q.21. . The extensions .gov, .edu, .mil, and .net are called.

A] DNSs.

B] E-mail targets.

C] Domain codes.

D] Mail to address.

Q.22. Web spiders and crawlers are examples of

A] Browsers.

B] Search Engines.

C] HTML Programs.

D] Flames.

Q.23. What is an URL ?

A] A software package used to cruise the World Wide Web..

B] The address of a resource on the World Wide Web.

C] The terms used to describe an internal wizard.

D] A live chat program [Unlimited real time language.

Q.24. What does the abbreviation "www." stands for.

A] World Wide Web.

B] Wide Wide Web.

C] World Width Web.

D] World with Web.

Q.25. Website that allows the user to search for data on keywords is:

A] Chat engines.

B] Routers.

C] Web Server.

D] Search engines.

Q.26. Which of the following web search engine is used worldwide?

A] Domain.

B] Google.

C] Toggle.

D] None of these.

Q.27. When you use a(n) .... to search for a topic, the information you search through is organized into a database like structure.

A] Search engine.

B] Index.

C] Spider.

D] Applet.

Q.28. Which of the following system electronic letter or message sent between individuals or computers.

A] E-mail.

B] Online Service.

C] Share Resources.

D] Voice mail messaging.

Q.29. To add current web to the favourites list.

A] Click "Favourites - Add to Favourites".

B] Click "Add - Favourites.

C] Click "File - Favourites.

D] All of these.

Q.30. Moving around the web from one site to another is referred to as................

A] Linking.

B] Navigating.

C] Hopping.

D] Paging.

Q.31. A protocol defines the rules for passing information between two or more computers.

A] True.

B] False.

Q.32. Information sent over the Internet is divided into small pieces called.

A] Packets.

B] PPPs.

C] e-mail forms.

D] Messages.

Q.33. Protocols like PPP and SLIP are used for.

A] Data Transfer.

B] Dialup internet connection.

C] Domain Registration.

D] None of these.

Q.34. The .com indicates websites of............. Types of organization.

A] Commercial.

B] Complex.

C] Company.

D] Cargo.

Q.35. Sending messages on the internet to another person's mailbox is

A] E-Business.

B] E-Letter.

C] E-Mail.

D] Cyber Mali.

Q.1. This is a type of personal information managers.

A] MS Word 2007

B] MS Excel 2007

C] MS PowerPoint 2007

D] MS Outlook 2007

Q.2. You can attach all sorts of files to an e-mail including Spreadsheets, word processor document database, even sound recordings and graphic images.

A] True

B] False

Q.3. To create a mail, We click on "Mail in the navigation pane.

A] True

B] False

Q.4. You uses the "Send/Receive" button to Send and receive mails.

A] True.

B] False.

Q.5. If you want to personalize your work environments wish to use a tool that organizes your contacts. Schedules etc. You will use.

A] Microsoft Office Excel 2007

B] Microsoft Office PowerPoint 2007

C] Microsoft Office Outlook 2007

D] Microsoft Office Word 2007

Q.6. Entry in MS Outlook 2007, that losts for more than 24 hours is called as

A] Event

B] Exhibition

C] Mail

D] Calendar

Q.7. Creating a Mail massage is also known as "Consolidating" a mail.

A] True.

B] False.

Q.8. The most important feature of outlook 2007 is sending and receiving an e-mail.

A] True.

B] False.

Q.9. A .... is a descriptive keyboard or phrase used in MS Outlook 2007 in which you can assign related items.

A] Category

B] Mail

C] Notes

D] Point

Q.10. Sourting tasks are the process of rearranging items in ascending order.

A] True.

B] False.

Q.11. The "Notebook" is an electronic book. which includes detailed information of all the people with whom you communicate.

A] True.

B] False.

Q.12. .... are separate external files that are along with you e-mail message.

A] Attachments

B] Options

C] E-mails

D] Parcels

Q.13. A task is a personal work related action item.

A] True.

B] False.

Q.14. The "Instant Search" Feature helps you to quickly find items in Microsoft Office Outlook 2007.

A] True.

B] False.

Q.15. In MS Outlook 2007 you can update the status of the tasks at any time and specify and percentage completed.

A] True.

B] False.

Q.16. If you add a recipient's name using "BCC" the name is not Visible to other recipients of the message.

A] True.

B] False.

Q.17. When you start Microsoft Outlook 2007. All the mails that you receive gets deposited in your "Inbox" Folder as default.

A] True.

B] False.

Q.18. Once We click on the flag symbol next to an important mail it gets added in the To Do Bar.

A] True.

B] False.

Q.19. You may need to save your contacts to a file, so that are available for use in the future. This is called.................

A] "Saving"

B] "Importing"

C] "Exporting"

D] "Extracting"

Q.20. A Mailing list is a collection of contacts.

A] True.

B] False.

Q.21. To Forward that mail that you have received, click on the mail from the inbox and then click the "Forward" button.

A] True.

B] False.

Q.22. "Notes" are an electronic version of paper notes that you use to go down quick reminders.

A] True

B] False

Q.23. If you add a recipient's name using "Cc", the name is not visible to other recipients of the message.

A] True.

B] False.

Q.24. When you open Microsoft Outlook 2007, you will see a navigation pane on the left. Which contains catefories such as mail, calender and contacts etc?

A] True.

B] False.

Q.25. In the Tasks Timeline view in MS Outlook 2007. The tasks are arranged according to their due dates.

A] True.

B] False.

Q.26. Sorting "Categories" is the process of rearranging items in ascending or descending order.

A] True.

B] False.

Q.27. In MS Outlook 2007 you may add contacts form different books into your mailing list.

A] True.

B] False.

Q.28. When you went to convey the information that you have received to your friend or any other person you may .... the mail that you have received.

A] "Share"

B] "Give"

C] "Send"

D] "Forward"

Q.29. "Cc" stands for carbon copy and "Bcc" stands for blind carbon copy.

A] True.

B] False.

Q.30. The .... is an electronic book, which includes detailed information of all the people with whom you communicate.

A] Address book

B] Calendar

C] Task

D] Notebook

Q.31. You can use a flag to quickly create a follow-up item that can be tracked in the To-Do-Bar, in your Inbox, and even in he calendar.

A] True.

B] False.

Q.32. You can sort your tasks in MS Outlook 2007 according to subject by selecting "View Arrange By Subject".

A] True.

B] False.

Q.33. When you start Microsoft Outlook 2007, all the mails that you receive get deposited in your "Drafts" folder as default.

A] True.

B] False.

Q.1. When a web site is developed; the various interlinked files are grouped together. This is achieved using which facility.

A] Hypertext.

B] Hyperlinks.

C] Network.

D] None of these.

Q.2. What does the abbreviation "www" in internet stands for:

A] World Wide Web.

B] Wide Wide Web.

C] World Width Web.

D] World with Web.

Q.3. .... is one of the fastest growing internet applications.

A] E-mail.

B] Shopping.

C] Investing.

D] Commerce.

Q.10. E-mail includes all of the following basic elements except.

A] Header.

B] Footer.

C] Message.

D] Signature.

Q.11. Instant messaging allows you

A] Send E-mail messages.

B] Sharing the data.

C] Instant reply of your messages.

D] To communicate with many at once in a conversation that occurs in real time.

Q.12.] When you use a] n. .... to search for a topic the information you search through is organized into a database - like structure.

A] Search Engine.
B] Index.
C] Spider.
D] Applet.
Q.13. .The extensions .gov, .edu, .mil, and .net are called.
A] DNSs.
B] E-mail targets.
C] Domain codes.
D] Mail to addresses.
Q.14.] Web spider are also known as search engines..
A] True.
B] False.
Q.15.B2c, C2C and B2B are types of...............
A] E-mail.
B] E-commerce.
C] E-cash.
D] All of these.
Q.16. For navigating any website, user has to enter.
A] URL.
B] www.
C] PPP.
D] None of these.
Q.17. Web spiders and Crawlers are examples of
A] Browsers.
B] Search Engines.
C] HTML Programs.
D] Flames.
Q.18. The .com indicates website of .... type of organization.
A] Commerce.
B] Complex.
C] Company.
D] Cargo.
Q.19.ISP stands for.
A] Internal Service Plan.
B] Internet Service Plan.
C] Integral Service Plan.
D] Internet Service Provider.
Q.20............ are programs that provide access to web resources.

A] Browsers.

B] Search Engines.

C] Programs.

D] All of these.

Q.21. Which is a web search engine used World Wide?

A] Domains.

B] Google.

C] Toggle.

D] All of these.

Q.22. Discussion on the internet about specific is known as

A] News.

B] News Group.

C] Veronica.

D] Telnet.

Q.23. Full from of URL

A] Universal Resource Locator.

B] Uniform Resource Locator.

C] Uni Resource Locator.

D] None of these.

Q.4. The keys labelled 0 -9 on the keyboard are called.

A] Function Keys.

B] Typewriters Keys.

C] Numeric Keys.

D] Special purpose Keys.

Q.5. The functions of a mouse and a track ball are different.

A] True.

B] False.

Q.6. .... devices translate what people understand into a form that computers can process.

A] Input.

B] Output.

A] All of these.

B] None of these.

Q.7. The keyboards keys that are labelled F1, F2 and so on are called................

A] Function Keys.

B] Numeric Keys.

C] Typewriter Keys.

D] Special Purpose Key.

Q.8. Which of the following device is not from pointing type of device?

A] Mouse.

B] Touch screen.

C] Key board.

D] Joystick.

Q.9. which of these is not a input device?

A] Monitor.

B] Mouse.

C] Key board.

D] Joystick.

Q.9. A CD-ROM stands for.

A] Compact Disk Read Only Memory.

B] Compact Disk Read Once Memory.

C] CD-RW.

D] None of these.

Q.10........... Programs that guard your computer system against viruses or other damaging programs.

A] Backup.

B] Anti Virus.

C] Uninstall.

D] None of these.

Q.11. What is the name given to a part of circle on which data is written in a storage media ?

A] Track.

B] Sector.

C] Cylinder.

D] Spiral.

Q.12. A CD-RW Disk means.

A] CD-Rewriteable.

B] CD-Recordable.

C] CD-ROM.

D] None of these.

Q.13. .... are produced by omega and topically have a 100 MB, 250 MB or 750 MB capacity over 500 times as much as today's standard floppy disk.

A] Super Disk.

B] HiFD Disk.

C] Zip Disk.

D] None of these.

Q.14. Primary storage is a volatile.

A] True.

B] False.

Q.15. HiFD Disks from the Sony Corporation have a capacity of 200 MB or 720 MB.

A] True.

B] False.

Q.16........... are produced by Imation and have a 120 MB or 240 MB capacity.

A] Super Disk.

B] HiFD Disk.

C] Zip Disk.

D] None of these.

Q.17. .... are removable storage devices used to store massive amounts of information.

A] Hard Disk Packs.

B] C.D..

C] Floppy Disk.

D] None of these.

Q.18. each track is divided into wedge-shaped sections called sectors.

A] True.

B] False.

Q.19. Storage device are hardware that reads data and programs from storage media.

A] True.

B] False.

Q.20. The 2 HD on a disk label means.

A] Two side, Low Density.

B] Two Side High Density.

C] One Side High Density.

D] None of these.

Q.21............ disks have a 120 MB storage capacity and the drivers are also able to read and store data on a standard 3.5" floppy disk.

A] Super Disks.

B] HiFD Disks.

C] Zip Disks.

D] None of these.

Q.22. Zip disks are produced by omega and typically have a 100 MB, 250 MB or 750 MB capacity over 500 times such as much as today's standard floppy disks.

A] True.

B] False.

Q.23. A CD-R stands for.

A] CD-Recordable.

B] CD-Runner.

C] CD-Receiver.

D] None of these.

Q.24. Each track is divided into wedge-shaped sections called.

A] Track.

B] Sectors.

C] Round.

D] None of these.

Q.25. Hard disk packs are removable storage devices used to massive amounts of information.

A] True.

B] False.

Q.26. Secondary Storage is non-volatile.

A] True.

B] False.

Q. 1 _______ is the practice and precautions taken to protect valuable information from unauthorized access, recording, disclosure or destruction.

A] Network Security

B] Database Security

C] Information Security

D] Physical Security

Q. 2 _______ platforms are used for safety and protection of information in the cloud.

A] Cloud workload protection platforms

B] Cloud security protocols

C] AWS

D] One Drive

Q. 3 Compromising confidential information comes under__

A] Bug

B] Threat

C] Vulnerability

D] Attack

Q. 4 An attempt to harm, damage or cause threat to a system or network is broadly termed as ______

A] Cyber-crime

B] Cyber Attack

C] System hijacking

D] Digital crime

Q. 5 The CIA triad is often represented by which of the following?

A] Triangle

B] Diagonal

C] Ellipse

D] Circle

Q. 6 Related to information security, confidentiality is the opposite of which of the following?

A] Closure

B] Disclosure

C] Disaster

D] Disposal

Q. 8 _______ means the protection of data from modification by unknown users.

A] Confidentiality

B] Integrity

C] Authentication

D] Non-repudiation

Q. 9 _______ of information means, only authorized users are capable of accessing the information.

A] Confidentiality

B] Integrity

C] Non-repudiation

D] Availability

Q. 10 This helps in identifying the origin of information and authentic user. This referred to here as __________

A] Confidentiality

B] Integrity

C] Authenticity

D] Availability

Q. 11 Data __________ is used to ensure confidentiality.

A] Encryption

B] Locking

C] Decryption

D] Backup

More MCQ Question Answers about Employability Skills

1] The plumber ------------ the pipes yesterday.

A] repair

B] repaired

C] was repair

D] was repaired

Answer= D

2] Kumar ---------- a good carpenter.

A] are

B]can

C]be

D]is

Answer= D

3] Come tomorrow and fix the door knoThis sentence is --------

A]interrogative

B]imperative

C]exclamatory

D]none

Answer= B

4] How effective the CTS training has been! This sentence is _________

A]exclamatory

B]imperative

C]declarative

D]none

Answer= A

5] While addressing your boss, you should be ------------.

A] Impolite

B] informal

C] formal

D] none

Answer= C

6] The customer requested the lady executive to display the

different mobile phone models. The customer asked ------- to mention the cost of the mobiles too.

A] him
B] his
C] her
D] It
Answer= C
7]The ITI Principal called Manoj. The Principal asked ------- to show ----- hall ticket for the CTS examination.
A] him,
B]his him,
C]her her,
D]his her,
Answer= A
8] Hi, how are you? What's up? – These are examples of ------------.
A] formal communication
B] informal communication
C] polite communication
D] none
Answer= B
9] How do you come to work? What is your qualification? – These are examples of ------------.
A] formal communication
B] informal communication
C] impolite communication
D] Improper communication
Answer= A
10] If you meet your supervisor in the grocery store, you will -----------.
A] turn your face and go away
B] run to him/her and hug him/her
C] greet him/her formally
D] greet him/her informally
Answer= C
11] When you borrow a screwdriver from a trainee, you should say, '--------
A] Give me your screwdriver
B] Can you give me your screwdriver?
C] What a nice screwdriver you have!
D] Spare me your screwdriver
Answer= B

12] The company asked the carpenter to design a box with the given dimensions. When it was approved, he made many more -------------- for the company.

A] box

B] cabinets

C] boxes

D] numbers

Answer= C

13] Magnificent, large, thin, lengthy, square, bright, sharp, hard are examples of ------------.

A] describing words

B] action words

C] pronouns

D] naming words

Answer= A

14] Table, wire, socket, cable, hammer, nail, pipe, motor, refrigerator – are examples of ------------.

A] action words

B] pronouns

C] describing words

D] naming words

Answer= D

15] Fix, measure, pull, lift, grind, mix, operate – are examples of -----------.

A] Vpronouns

B] action words

C] describing words

D] naming words

Answer= B

16] Commas, full stops, question marks – are examples of ------------.

A] design

B] punctuation marks

C] formal communication

D] none

Answer= B

17] You are requested to complete the given assignment by Monday. This is an example of ----------------.

A] impolite communication

B] formal communication

C] informal communication

D] oral communication

Answer= B

18] Gestures, facial expressions, eye contact are examples of ------------.

A] verbal communication

B] non-verbal communication

C] acting skills

D] communication skills

Answer= B

19] I have received complaints about workplace safety.

Please check them immediately and share the details with me. This is an example of ------------.

A] casual communication

B] formal workplace communication

C] informal communication

D] informal workplacecommunication

Answer= B

20] Greetings help you to ------------.

A] establish a connection with someone you meet in formal and informal situations.

B] establish a connection with someone you meet in formal situations.

C] establish a connection with someone you meet in informal situations.

D] establish cordial relationship

Answer= A

21] When you meet the instructor inside or outside the ITI, it is ------------.

A] always formal

B] always informal

C] formal inside the ITI

D] informal outside the ITI

Answer= A

22] In the context of an interview --------------- greetings is to be used.

A] formal

B] informal

C] friendly

D] cordial

Answer= A

23] When you make an enquiry at a bank, it is ------------------situation.

A] an informal

B] a formal

C] a friendly

D] a casual

Answer= B

24 During the COVID-19 pandemic, it is better to --------- than shake hands, and say Namaste than ---

A] hug,

B] wave hands wave hands,

C] hug hold hands,

D] hug none

Answer= B

25] A good -------------------------- helps to create a good first impression.

A] family

B] friend

C] self-introduction

D] all of the above

Answer= C

26] We may have to introduce colleagues, peers and superiors in ------------------- context.

A] self-introduction

B] informal

C] formal

D] official

C

27] A quick self-introduction is called --------------

A] elevation pitch

B] elevator tone

C] elevator pitch

D] elevation tone

Answer= C

28] When you attend a friend's wedding with your father, you may have to introduce your father to your friend and your friend to your father. What kind of situation is it?

A] elevator pitch

B] formal

C] informal

D] elevation tone

Answer= C

29] As a customer sales executive in an electrical appliances showroom, your greetings and introduction of your instructor to your supervisor shall be ________

A] descriptive

B] formal

C] informal

D] elevator tone

Answer= B

30] -------------------- are persons with very good behaviour, achievements and lead as an example.

A] customer service executives

B] sales supervisors

C] ITI instructors

D] role models

Answer= D

31] Role models -------------------------- people to follow them.

A] elevate

B] instruct

C] inspire

D] none

Answer= C

34] The set of imperfections in a person is called --------------------

A] Strengths

B] elevations

C] imitations

D] weaknesses

Answer= D

37] When we greet our superiors, managers and boss we greet them ----------------------.

A] informally

B] casually

C] formally

D] indifferently

Answer= C

39] What we communicate without words, but with body language is an example of ---------------------

A] verbal communication
B] formal communication
C] informal communication
D] non-verbal communication
Answer= D

40 Working with others to find a mutually agreeable solution is called ----------------------

A] persuasion
B] communication
C] negotiation
D] assertion
Answer= C

42] 'Good morning', 'nice to meet you', 'How have you been?' are examples of ---------------

A] formal greetings
B] informal greetings
C] superiors
D] organizations
Answer= A

43 Writing emails, letters, memos, orders, filling forms,
minutes, contracts, proposals and quotations are examples
of ---------------------------- workplace communication.

A] informal
B] non-verbal
C] formal
D] verbal
Answer= B

44] Writing a leave letter is part of -------------------------communication.

A] formal workplace
B] informal workplace
C] non-verbal workplace
D] none
Answer= A

50] ------------ means the immediate surroundings to the place one lives in.

A] Workplace
B] Facilities
C] City

D] Neighbourhood

Answer= D

52] We -------------------- books from a library.

A] buy

B] sell

C] borrow

D] none

Answer= C

54] The area is --------------------- as the houses in it cost a lot of money.

A] beautiful

B] expensive

C] safe

D] big

Answer= B

55] There are --------------------- apartments in my neighbourhood.

A] spacious

B] school

C] kind

D] fresh

Answer= A

56] It is a ---------------------- locality. One need not fear.

A] boring

B] safe

C] school

D] fresh

Answer= B

57] There is water scarcity in the locality. The area is -------------.

A] polluted

B] noisy

C] dry

D] uneven

Answer= C

58 Transportation to some rural areas is difficult as the roads are -----------.

A] polluted

B] dry

C] spacious

D] uneven

Answer= D

59 There is a big playground ----------------------- our house.

A] on

B] in

C] near

D] over

Answer= C

60 There is a garden with ----------------- flowers in our neighbourhood.

A] safe

B] clear

C] lovely

D] none

Answer= C

66 Rainwater harvesting ---------------------- to prevent water scarcity.

A] gives

B] gave

C] help

D] helps

Answer= D

71 ---------------------------- the computer every day after use.

A] Turn on

B] Switch on

C] Turn off

D] all of the above

Answer= C

73 Gardening, reading, collecting stamps, singing ---------------some examples of hobbies.

A] is

B] was

C] were

D] are

Answer= D

74 The Jog falls is the second ----------------------- waterfall in India.

A] tallest

B] highest

B] higher

C] taller

Answer= B

75 The world's ---------------------- beach is along the Bay of Bengal in Tamil Nadu.

A] highest

B] longer

C] longest

D] high

Answer= C

76 One of the seven ------------- of the modern world is located in Agra in Uttar Pradesh.

A] wonder

B] wander

C] wanders

D] wonders

Answer= D

96 The singular form of lenses is_____

A] Lens

B] Len

C] Lense

D] Lenses

Answer= A

97 Which word is an adjective_____

A] Beautiful

B] Park

C] Wave

D] Sea

Answer= A

98 Miscommunication can lead to ----------------.

A] Build relationships

B] Create misunderstanding

C] Successful Planning

D] See effective results

Answer= B

99 For effective communication ----------------.

A] Keep Listening.

B] Keep Talking.

C] Listen and talk carefully.

D] Listen carefully but talk unnecessarily.

Answer= C

100 Primary storage devices are -----------------

A] DVD

B] CD

C] RAM,

D] USB

Answer= C

101 What is stress?

A] Feeling of joy

B] Feeling of surprise

C] Feeling of delight

D] Feeling of frustration/disappointment

Answer= D

102 How many days does it take to form a habit?

A] 10

B] 11

C] 15

D] 21

Answer= D

103 Factories Act was introduced in -----------------.

A] 1948

B] 1956

C] 1949

D] 1980

Answer= A

104 Wages are paid -----------------.

A] Daily

B] Monthly

C] Quarterly

D] Yearly

Answer= B

105 When a worker contributes to bring the best output by using the available resources, the worker is -----------------.

A] Productive

B] effective

C] Reliable

D] Selfish

Answer= A

106 PPE means -----------------.

A] Personal Productive Equipment
B] Personal Protective Equipment
C] Productive Personal Equipment
D] Personal Protective Engine
Answer= B

107 Productivity can be increased by offering ----------------.
A] Training only
B] Jobsite Experience only
C] Training and Jobsite Experience
D] Incentive
Answer= C

108 ---------------- protect hands from cuts, burns or harmful liquids.
A] Goggles
B] Gloves
C] Ear plugs
D] Helmets
Answer= B

109 Which of these is not an entry level job after ITI for interior designers?
A] Specialist
B] Interns
C] Junior Interior Designer
D] Design Assistant
Answer= A

110 Quality Management system makes use of some tools for problem solving. Which of the following is not one of them?
A] fishbone diagrams
B] 5D and 5S methods
C] 4D and 4S methods
D] Kaizen principle
Answer= C

111 ISO stands for ---------------- .
A] International Order for Standardization
B] International Organizers for Standardization
C] International Organization for Stabilization
D] International Organization for Standardization
Answer= D

112 BIS stands for ---------------- .

A] Bureau of Indian Standards

B] Bureau of International Standards

C] Bureau of Indian States

D] Board of Indian Standards

Answer= A

113 The business idea should ---------------- .

A] Satisfy only my needs

B] Solve someone's problem

C] Save the world

D] None of the above

Answer= B

114 In social media, we use ----------- to convey our feelings and emotions.

A] emoji's

B] gestures

C] eye contact

D] bodily movements

Answer= A

115 We select the ----------------------- emoji to express our feelings.

A] random

B] perfect

C] odd

D] none

Answer= B

117 When we strongly feel or react situations or with particular people, we are using our --------------

A] emotions

B] health

C] money

D] none

A

118 It is important to ----------------------.

A] accept, understand and manage our emotions

B] accept, misunderstand and manage our emotions

C] refuse, misunderstand and manage our emotions

D] accept and misunderstand emotions

Answer= A

119 A person's ability to understand and manage emotions properly is called ----------------------.

A] Intelligence Artificial

B] intelligence Emotional

C] Intelligence

D] split personality

Answer= C

120 A person with high emotional intelligence has -----------------.

A] lot of negative qualities

B] ego

C] lot of positive qualities

D] a job

Answer= C

122 The first step to manage emotions is to ----------------------. accept and

A] understand emotions

B] express emotions

C] manage emotions

D] reject emotions

Answer= A

126 What is the process of formally introducing oneself called?

A] hiring

B] decision

C] self-introduction

D] seeking

Answer= C

127 A good self-introduction will help in making a ---------------decision.

A] chatting

B] transfer

C] hiring

D] family

Answer= C

128 All of us -------------------- on completion of the course.

A] feel bored

B] search for jobs

C] feel relaxed

D] feel free

Answer= B

130 Good self-introduction help to make ----------------------

A] negative impression

B] money good

C] positive impression

D] offer of appointment

Answer= C

131 Self-introduction should show how ---------------------- your are.

A] dull

B] confident

C] angry

D] weak

Answer= B

132 A quick summary of yourself is called an ----------------------.

A] angry tone

B] easy speech

C] elevator pitch

D] emotional talk

Answer= C

134 The most frequently asked question in an interview is-----------------

A] tell me about yourself

B] Feedback

C] what is quarantine?

D] where is my pen?

Answer= A

135 Everything about a person on the internet like profile on Facebook, Twitter and Instagram is called ----------------------

A] online profile or digital

B] footprint

C] social media ecosystem

D] networking

Answer= A

136 Identify the professional networking platform from the given options.

A] Facebook

B] Snapchat

C] LinkedIn

D] WhatsApp

Answer= C

137 When you explore LinkedIn to know about companies, its employers, get industry updates, etc., you are exploring it -----

A] none

B] networking

C] building your brand

D] as a research tool

Answer= D

138 When a person is given information about how he/she is doing in an effort to reach a goal, it is called --------------------.

A] verification

B] argument

C] feedback

D] frightening

Answer= C

139 Giving information in a manner that does not attack a person, but brings possible changes to the behaviour is called ---------------------.

A] suggestion

B] pleasing

C] effective feedback

D] none

Answer= C

140 When your instructor decides to cancel the industry visit, you feel---------

A] Feel confused

B] Feel disappointed

C] Feel stressed

D] jump in happiness

Answer= B

141 When others observe you and share what they feel about your performance, they -----------

A] want to make you feel bad

B] don't like you

C] are your enemies

D] are giving you feedback for improvement

Answer= D

142 An employee gets feedback from supervisors, HR and other colleagues to

A] improve

B] feel bad
C] be insulted
D] feel uncomfortable
Answer= A

143 Negative feedback is usually given ---------------------.
A] Constructively
B] to discourage
C] to hurt the receiver
D] to demoralize
Answer= A

144 To improve your listening skills and become a better communicator, you need to ---------------
A] start listening actively
B] ignore listening
C] be indifferent
D] listen partially
Answer= A

145 "Your assignment is not like that of the others in your class. Why aren't you studying?" is an example of --------------------
A] positive feedback
B] encouraging comments
C] negative feedback
D] usual comment
Answer= C

146 Giving positive comments followed by suggestions for improvement and closing with positive comments is called ------------.
A] negative feedback
B] listening technique
C] Burger feedback technique
D] Positive feedback
Answer= C

147 When you provide feedback, tell the listener that you are providing -------.
A] negative feedback
B] comments
C] constructive feedback for improvement
D] suggestions
Answer= C

148 Self-reflection is the process of ---------------------.
A] commenting
B] looking inwards
C] feedback
D] looking forward
Answer= B
149 When we take time to think and pay attention to our thoughts, emotions, decisions, and behaviour, it is called ---
A] constructive criticism
B] positive feedback
C] negative feedback
D] self-reflection
Answer= D
150 Identifying things that are under our control and those that are not under our control, helps us to be ---------------------
A] more self-aware
B] peaceful
C] none
D] discouraged
Answer= A
151 Official conversations are part of ---------------------.
A] informal communication
B] formal communication
C] resumes
D] families
Answer= B
152 Conversation between family members at home or casual conversation between employees is ---------------------.
A] formal communication
B] discussion
C] none
D] informal communication
Answer= D
153 Single strand communication, gossip, cluster and probability are examples of ---------------------.
A] informal communication
B] feedback
C] formal communication

D] burger feedback

Answer= A

154 Using words through speaking or writing to share information, thoughts or ideas is called ----------------------.

A] non-verbal communication

B] feedback

C] verbal communication

D] none

Answer= C

155 Good verbal communication ----------------------. helps to

A] communicate clearly

B] confuses people

C] is disrespectful

D] is rude

Answer= A

156 When we write letters, emails, messages, etc., we are using ---------------

A] employability

B] verbal communication

C] non-verbal communication

D] none

Answer= B

157 Communicating without words using only gestures, body language, facial expressions, etc., is called ----------------------

A] feedback

B] verbal communication

C] interviews

D] non-verbal communication

Answer= D

158 The ability to rcccive and accurately interpret messages in the communication process is called -----------------.

A] listening

B] speaking

C] reading

D] writing

Answer= A

159 Good listening skills make workers -----------------. productive irresponsible crazy inefficient A

160 Listening to radio, television shows, etc., is an example of –

A] active listening

B] non-verbal communication

C] passive listening

D] verbal communication

Answer= B

161 Paying attention to the speaker, not interrupting, taking time to understand before asking questions or responding is -----------------.

A] passive listening

B] lecturing

C] active listening

D] accepting

Answer= C

162 When society decides how we need to behave and forces it on us, it is called creating ----------

A] free society

B] equality gender

C] stereotypes

D] enforcement

Answer= C

164 An important document to carry when attending an interview is

A] cover letter

B] resume

C] leave letter

D] none

Answer= B

165 A --------------------- is a summary of your

A] Personal experience,

B] skills and education history.

C] feedback letter

D] resume story

Answer= C

166 The crucial step that all face while starting their careers is –

A] feeling happy

B] facing an interview

C] going on a tour

D] relaxing

Answer= B

168 Customers generally ---------------- when they have a poor experience.

A] recommend to friends

B] continue doing business with the company

C] switch to a competitor

D] bargain with the company

Answer= C

169 An employee comes late to the office every day. He is not –

A] silent

B] punctual

C] confident

D] clean

Answer= B

171 The electronic form of formal written communication that can be sent through the internet to many people across the world is called --------------.

A] email

B] typing

C] printing

D] writing

Answer= A

172 The most effective way of formal communication is -----------

A] chatting

B] tweeting

C] typing

D] email

Answer= D

173 CC in email means ----------------------.

A] chair copy

B] child copy

C] carbon copy

D] chart copy

Answer= C

174 BCC in email means ----------------------.

A] blind chair copy

B] blind child copy

C] blind chart copy

D] blind carbon copy

Answer= D

175 When you send your resume through email, you are sending it as ---------

A] driver attachment

B] marked text

C] cookie

D] advertisement

Answer= B

176 When your classmate is giving suggestions on your performance, you are receiving ----------------

A] customer interaction

B] elevator pitch

C] feedback

D] an award

C

177 PowerPoint files have -------------- extensions.

A].doc

B].xls

C] .jpg

D] .pptx

Answer= D

178 Shortcut keys Ctrl+C, Ctrl+V, Ctrl+S mean ---------------------.

A] save, cut, copy

B] cut, save, copy

C] copy, paste, save

D] cut, copy, save

Answer= C

179 Pressing Esc in PowerPoint can ---------------------.

A] add a new slide

B] start slide show

C] end slide show

D] create a new presentation

Answer= C

180 To create a new presentation, choose ---------------------.

A] Ctrl+C

B] Ctrl+V

C] Ctrl+B

D] Ctrl+N

Answer= D

182 The most compatible format for saving images is ----------------.

A] Pdf

B] JPG

C] xls

D] doc

Answer= B

183 Excel is used to ----------------------.

A] save and share documents of all sizes

B] create typed document files

C] create spreadsheet with various functions

D] create presentations for a wide range of fields

Answer= C

185 JPG means ----------------------.

A] Junior Photography Group

B] Joint Photo Group

C] Joint Photographic Group

D] Junior Photographic Group

Answer= C

186 SVG file means ----------------------.

A] Scalable Venn Graphics file

B] Senior Vector Graphics

C] Scalable Venn Glitz

D] Scalable Vector Graphics

Answer= D

187 Participants in live seminars and discussions can ----------- when it is enabled.

A] information

B] view

C] interact

D] listen

Answer= C

188 Wi-Fi stands for ------------------------------------ wireless signal.

A] Wireless Fidelity

B] Wireless Finish

C] Wireless Filament

D] Wireless Firmament

Answer= A

189 ----- is a wireless technology standard used for exchanging data between fixed and mobile devices over short distances.

A] Wi-Fi

B] webcasting

C] Bluetooth

D] email

Answer= C

190 When we share photos and videos from our Android smartphones to the computer to see them on a larger screen we are ---------------------.

A] telecasting

B] screen mirroring

C] zooming media

D] zooming

Answer= B

191 A ---------------- is a computer that provides data to other computers.

A] Smartphone

B] laptop

C] modem

D] Server

Answer= D

193 The image of the cloud is often used to refer to --------------

A] internet

B] server

C] data

D] text

Answer= A

194 To retrieve photos and videos from Facebook, we need to have a ---------

A] personal server

B] device with internet connection

C] hard disk

D] printer

Answer= B

196 Siri and Alexa are called_________

A] machines

B] smart assistants

C] predictors

D] recorder

Answer= B

197 An important aspect of being a successful entrepreneur is___________

A] Having an entrepreneurial mindset

B] Earning money

C] Serving the society

D] Expanding to as many markets as possible

Answer= A

198 Knowing what you are good at and what you need to improve on is the quality of______

A] Self-awareness

B] Self-belief

C] Independent decision

D] Making Grit

Answer= A

199 Taking decisions on your own, after carefully thinking about them is the quality of_______

A] Self-awareness

B] Self-belief

C] Independent decision

D] Making Grit

Answer= C

200 What is a prototype?

A] The business idea

B] Typing the product/service in the business plan

C] Selling the product/service

D] The first version of a product/service

Answer= D

201 One important rule to network effectively is_________ talk to the same people keep in touch with your

A] contacts

B] focus on selling

C] your product

D] identify your competitors

Answer= B

202 Networking is__________

A] making new enemies

B] identifying your competition
C] making connections with other businesses and customers
D] joining a social network
Answer= C

205 Anitha started an Instagram page for her crafts business. She used ________ marketing strategy
A] online marketing
B] taglines
C] poster
D] Networking
Answer= A

206 Human resources are__________
A] your neighbours
B] your staff,
C] employees and other helpers
D] your customers your competitors
Answer= B

207 Which of the following is not a resource?
A] raw materials
B] customer database
C] profit earned
D] your bed
Answer= D

208 When you have confidence in your own abilities and trust in yourself, you have
A] open mindedness
B] Proactiveness
C] belief in yourself
D] optimism
Answer= C

209 You are a lifelong learner if you________
A] get a PhD
B] make a lot of money
C] live for a long time
D] keep growing and adding to your knowledge
Answer= D

210 One of the benefits of being a lifelong learner is_______
A] becoming a better decision maker

B] becoming famous

C] making lots of friends

D] staying physically fit

Answer= A

212 Maintaining the quality of something at a certain level is called

A] communication

B] problem solving

C] sustainability

D] interaction

Answer= C

218 The work undertaken by a person for a period of time is called________

A] job

B] career

C] planning

D] expert

Answer= A

219 Any task or piece of work for which a person gets paid for is called a_____

A] Career

B] projection

C] job

D] plan

Answer= C

220 When a carpenter makes a wooden chair and gets paid for it, it is his_________

A] plan

B] joy

C] job

D] career

Answer= C

222 Career is like a long train journey where ----------------------- are the many stations, many stops, many changes in routes.

A] plans

B] jobs

C] grows

D] Dreams

Answer= B

225 The materials and support that you need to complete your milestones on time is called ____

A] Timelines

B] Resources

C] status

D] descriptions

Answer= A

226 Setting up date for completing each milestone is called________

A] descriptions

B] resource

C] timeline

D] None

Answer= C

227 We need to have----------------- when market trends change or when our current job no longer exists.

A] career paths

B] models

C] alternative careers

D] payment

Answer= C

228 When you know how to stitch a garment by hand, learning how to do it using a machine is called_______

A] career

B] employment

C] upskilling

D] learning

Answer= C

230 Trying new things and finding new ways to do old things is called___________

A] negotiation

B] collaboration

C] innovation

D] Communication

Answer= C

231 We--------------- in a proper way so that we may reach a profitable and healthy compromise.

A] Collaborate

B] negotiate

C] innovate

D] elevate

Answer= B

232 Thinking in a smart way by questioning the information you receive so that you are not fooled by fake news is called____________

A] negotiation

B] innovation

C] career

D] critical thinking

Answer= D

233 The ability to adapt to fast changes is___________

A] innovation

B] negotiation

C] collaboration

D] adaptability

Answer= D

234 When we work with others, it is called____________

A] innovation

B] career

C] collaboration

D] Decision-making

Answer= C

236 A person who learns new things related to his/her career and is up-to-date with latest industrial developments has____________

A] stalled mindset

B] growth mindset

C] collaboration

D] communication

Answer= B

237 A person who does not take necessary steps to learn new skills even when there is threat of losing his/her job is_ _______

A] open-minded

B] not open-minded

C] adaptable

D] inefficient

Answer= B

238 The process of learning a completely new set of skills to perform a different type of a job is__________

A] upskilling

B] reskilling

C] ITI

D] Apprenticeship

Answer= B

239 If a woodcutter who so far used simple axe learns to use an electric axe, the woodcutter is__________

A] reskilling

B] career

C] critical

D] upskilling

Answer= D

243 The natural ability of a person to do something and how quickly he/she can learn something is called____________

A] upskilling

B] reskilling

C] career path

D] Aptitude

Answer= D

245 A man can reach a certain place in 40 hours. If he reduces his speed by $1/15^{th}$, he goes 5 km less in that time. Find the total distance covered by him.

A] 60

B] 85

C] 75

D] 52

Answer= C

246 3 is what percentage of 3000?

A] 10%

B] 5%

C] 1%

D] 0.1%

Answer= D

247 A man bought a lamp for Rs 100 and sold it for Rs 120. How much profit did he make? What is the profit percentage?

A] Profit Rs 10; Profit percentage 40%

B] Profit Rs 20; Profit percentage 20%

C] Profit Rs 20; Profit percentage 10%

D] Profit Rs. 20; profit percentage 2%

Answer= B

248 Rehearsing or practice sessions before an interview is called______________

A] pre-interview

B] amateur rehearsal

C] post interview

D] mock interview

Answer= D

249 Activities that one does during free time such as reading, gardening, writing blogs are called___________

A] experience

B] hobbies

C] qualifications

D] Objectives

Answer= B

250 When a person is naturally good at doing something, it is his/her_____________

A] weakness

B] family

C] strengths

D] hereditary

Answer= C

251 Tools and techniques used to make one's task easier to work efficiently and mentioned in resumes are called___________

A] software

B] reading

C] examples

D] skills

Answer= D

252 A paid period of training that allows you to learn a particular skill or a set of skills while you work in the industry is called___________

A] crafting

B] opportunity

C] entrepreneurship

D] apprenticeship

Answer= D

255 Identify the professional networking platform from the given options.

A] Facebook

B] Instagram

C] Linked

D] LinkedIn

Answer= D

259 ICC with respect to POSH and sexual harassment means

A] Internal Cricket Committee

B] International Compliant Committee

C] Internal Company Committee

D] Internal Complaint Committee

Answer= D

260 .-------- means the practice of keeping yourself and your surroundings neat and clean.

A] health

B] safety

C] community

D] hygiene

Answer= D

261 Some examples of------------- hygiene are maintaining trimmed and clean nails, brushing teeth twice a day, washing hands before and after eating food.

A] Community

B] organisational

C] personal

D] Personnel

Answer= C

262 Taking care of the environment around us is called -----------hygiene

A] Community

B] organisational

C] personal

D] personnel

Answer= A

263 What is an essential life skill for social and professional purpose?

A] Learning English

B] Learning mother- tongue

C] Learning foreign language

D] Learning more language

Answer= A

264 While addressing your boss, you should be...

A] Impolite

B] Informal

C] Formal

D] Expressive

Answer= C

265 Hi, how are you, what is up, these are examples of....

A] formal communication

B] Informal communication

C] Polite communication

D] Impolite communication

Answer= B

266 What you say first when you meet someone?

A] Goodbye

B] Good day

C] See you

D] Good morning

Answer= D

268 Fill in the blank with correct past tense of the verb"I__________a movie yesterday"

A] Watch

B] am watching

C] watched

D] will watch

Answer= C

269 Singular form of devices is....

A] Devise

B] Divice

C] Divise

D] Device

Answer= D

270 "The announcement .... yesterday was unnecessary" complete the sentence with appropriate word.

A] Made

B] make

C] was made

D] will make

Answer= A

271 Fill in the blank with proper interrogative ....went wrong with yesterday's game.

A] Where

B] What

C] When

D] Who

Answer= B

273 Complete the sentence with appropriate word "The Plumber .... the tap only now.

A] Fit

B] are fitting

C] is fitting

D] was fitting

Answer= C

274 When you start a discussion on a topic, what do you say?

A] Let you start

B] let me say

C] let's discuss

D] let's us finish

Answer= C

275 What do you say when you politely disagree?

A] I'm afraid

B] I have to disagree.

C] you are wrong

D] he is right

Answer= A

276 Complete the sentence with suitable describing words.

The area is _______as the houses in it cost a lot of money.

A] beautiful

B] good

C] expensive

D] spacious

Answer= C

277 Complete the sentence with suitable describing words

The roads in my town are in _________ condition.

A] good

B] expensive
C] beautiful
D] safe
Answer= A
278 Complete the sentence with suitable describing words
There is a __________ garden with lovely flowers.
A] good
B] spacious
C] big
D] beautiful
Answer= D
279 Complete the sentence with suitable describing words
There is a _________ playground near our house.
A] spacious
B] big
C] beautiful
D] good
Answer= B
280 Complete the sentence with suitable describing words
There are _________ apartments in my neighbourhood.
A] expensive
B] beautiful
C] good
D] spacious
Answer= D
281 Complete the sentence with suitable describing words
It is a _________ neighbourhood. One need not fear.
A] good
B] big
C] safe
D] expensive
Answer= C
282 Complete the sentence with suitable describing words
There isn't any amusement park in the area. It is a ____place.
A] polluted
B] dry
C] noisy
D] boring

Answer= D

283 Complete the sentence with suitable describing words

There is a factory in the area. The air is ________.

A] polluted

B] boring

C] uneven

D] noisy

Answer= A

284 Complete the sentence with suitable describing words

There is water scarcity in the locality. The area is________.

A] uneven

B] noisy

C] dry

D] boring

Answer= C

285 Complete the sentence with suitable describing words

The transportation to some rural areas is difficult as the roads are__________

A] dry

B] polluted

C] even

D] uneven

Answer= D

286 What help us to maintain the balance between mental and physical activities?

A] Hobbies

B] Running

C] Walking

D] Reading

Answer= A

288 The immediate surroundings to the place you live in is called_____

A] village

B] town

C] city

D] neighbourhood

Answer= D

289 The conditions in a place that affect the behaviour and development of somebody or something is called__________

A] neighbourhood
B] environment
C] locality
D] facilities
Answer= B
291 which one is not an adventure?
A] climbing
B] mountains treaking
C] surfing
D] driving
Answer= D
292 Travelling in the sea is called a_____
A] voyage
B] boating
C] fishing
D] tour
Answer= A

www.ingramcontent.com/pod-product-compliance
Ingram Content Group UK Ltd.
Pitfield, Milton Keynes, MK11 3LW, UK
UKHW021910190726
13853UKWH00002B/610